QUILTS
for Red-Letter Days

More than 30 Small Celebration Quilts

That
Patchwork
Place®

Janet Kime

Acknowledgments

Many thanks to my friends Marilyn Bacon and Joel T. Patz, and to my sister Karen Gabriel, who donated their time and skills to the cause. Special thanks to Virginia Morrison, who was quilting right up to the eleventh hour; without her help and enthusiasm, this book would not have been possible.

Dedication

For Karen and Lois. Thanks for the idea.

Credits

Managing Editor . . . . .Greg Sharp
Technical Editor . . . . Ursula Reikes
Copy Editor . . . . Liz McGehee
Proofreader . . . . Melissa Riesland
Design Director . . . . Judy Petry
Text and Cover Designer . . . . Kay Green
Production Assistant . . . . Shean Bemis
Illustrator . . . . Brian Metz
Illustration Assistant . . . . Lisa McKenney
Photographer . . . . .Brent Kane
Photography Asssistant . . . . Richard Lipshay

Library of Congress Cataloging-in-Publication Data

Kime, Janet,
    Quilts for red-letter days : more than 30 small celebration quilts/ Janet Kime.
        p. cm.
    ISBN 1-56477-130-X
    1. Quilting—Patterns.   2. Patchwork—Patterns.
    3. Miniature quilts.   4. Holiday decorations.
    I. Title.
    TT835.K495 1996
    746.46'0433'0228—dc20   95-44951
                                                      CIP

Quilts for Red-Letter Days
©1996 by Janet Kime

 That
Patchwork
Place®

That Patchwork Place, Inc.
PO Box 118
Bothell, WA 98041-0118 USA

Printed in the United States of America
01 00 99 98 97 96   6 5 4 3 2 1

MISSION STATEMENT

WE ARE DEDICATED TO PROVIDING QUALITY PRODUCTS AND SERVICES THAT INSPIRE CREATIVITY.

WE WORK TOGETHER TO ENRICH THE LIVES WE TOUCH.

That Patchwork Place is a financially responsible ESOP company.

Table of Contents

Introduction

The quilts in this book are all small wall quilts, designed to be displayed on holidays or during particular seasons of the year. Most of them are not meant to be heirlooms; they are meant to be fun. Some of them are downright silly. Their very silliness can set you, the quilter, free. You can break all the rules with these quilts—and who cares? They will never be washed, so you can use oddball fabrics of unknown fiber and unpredictable behavior: blends, velvets, metallics, and laces. Need a print with dogs on it? Cruise the flannels, the corduroys, even the silkies.

You can glue things to the quilts if you don't feel like sewing them. You can use icky thread. You don't even have to quilt them if you don't want to; they are only 12" square.

The ones that were machine quilted were seldom basted first; usually, they were pinned together with straight pins, quilted a bit here and there, and then bound.

The quilts use a variety of techniques, some of which may be new to you. If you haven't tried foundation piecing yet, or appliqué with fusible web, or beading, this is the time to try these techniques. It's only a 12" quilt, so you aren't going to waste $50 worth of fabric. If you don't like a technique, you can probably grit your teeth long enough to finish a 12" square (and be glad you didn't promise to make a bedspread for your daughter). In many places, you can substitute one technique for another. If you don't have the patience to paper-patch sixty-four violet petals, fuse them to the background instead. If you don't like embroidery, use fabric paint.

If you make one of these quilts and aren't happy with it, try spraying glitter on it. Trust me—spray glitter is the fairy dust of the '90s, and it turns any quilt into a small celebration.

Quilting the Calendar

The idea for this book originated with my sister and her quilting buddy, who decided to make a series of 12"-square holiday quilts for their offices, one to hang on each holiday. My sister and I send each other "care packages" every few months. In her next box, I packed a 12" Presidents' Day quilt, a traditional block named Lincoln's Platform with a cherry-print border. It went together so quickly and was so pretty that I was captivated. I planned more surprise quilts, trying to think of holidays for which she would not already have made quilts. Soon I was scouring the library for information on holidays and found a truly wonderful book: *Chase's Calendar of Events*.

Chase's Calendar (Contemporary Books, Inc.), revised each year, is an immense and thoroughly indexed collection of historic events, anniversaries, birthdays, and local celebrations, many with a fascinating paragraph or so of information. I was off, surprising my sister (and bemusing her office mates) with quilts for Bastille Day, Kentucky Derby Day, Boss's Day, Grandparents' Day, and the often neglected annual return of the buzzards to Hinckley, Ohio.

This book includes quilts for most of the major holidays and seasons as well as some less well-known reasons to celebrate. These ideas are just a jumping-off point. There are many more holidays as well as personal events to celebrate, and many other possible quilts to celebrate them.

Major Holidays

Most libraries have a good selection of books about holiday celebrations. The best ones are books for children because they are full of pictures. Search under "Holiday" or ask a librarian to show you the area where holiday books are and then scan the titles.

Many holidays, seasons, and events can be represented with easily recognizable designs. There is no lack of Christmas or Halloween designs from which to choose. For ideas for these and other holidays, look at greeting cards, children's coloring books, wrapping paper, and holiday magazines.

Minor Holidays and Anniversaries

Books covering these celebrations will probably be in the reference section. Again, ask the librarian for help. You may not be able to check out new reference books, but you might be able to check out editions from past years. Some of these books are just lists. The ones with descriptions of holidays and events will provide more fuel for your imagination. The reference section might also include books about local fairs and festivals.

If you have a list of holidays but are not sure how to represent them in quilts, search further in the library. My prize find was a whole book about vultures, which helped me draw the birds in "Buzzards' Return." Again, the illustrations in books for children can be inspirational.

The Unusual and Downright Weird

Chase's Calendar is my favorite source for oddball celebrations. Do you know, for example, about Johnny Appleseed Day (March 11)? Do you know the actual date when the Pied Piper of Hamelin supposedly performed his magic (July 22, 1376)? Do you still have some of that Elvis Presley fabric? *Chase's* lists at least eight days on which you can hang a quilt celebrating the King. And what quilter doesn't have a UFO (unfinished object) suitable for hanging during National Procrastination Week (scheduled for the second week of March but often celebrated sometime later)? Entertain your family or office mates with decorations for unusual holidays.

Personal Celebrations

These can be the most fun. Make a birthday quilt for each family member. Do you and your partner have a special place, song, food, or joke? Make a quilt about it and hang it on an anniversary—or hang it anytime. Did your son letter in track? Is the dog finally trained? Did someone receive a promotion? Graduate? Get married? Is this the year you go to Paducah? Preserve your memories in little quilts.

Birthday Symbols

The following chart lists the flowers and gemstones associated with the birthdays for each month. Make birthday quilts from fabrics printed with the flowers, or use the flower or gemstone to determine the color scheme of a birthday quilt.

Month	Flower	Gemstone
January	carnation	garnet
February	violet, primrose	amethyst
March	daffodil	aquamarine, bloodstone
April	daisy, sweet pea	diamond
May	lily of the valley, hawthorn	emerald
June	rose	moonstone, pearl, alexandrite
July	larkspur, water lily	ruby
August	poppy, gladiola	sardonyx, peridot
September	morning glory, aster	sapphire
October	cosmos, calendula	opal, tourmaline
November	chrysanthemum	topaz
December	poinsettia, holly	zircon, turquoise

Traditional Block Designs

Many holidays can be represented by traditional blocks with related names. "Grandparents' Day" on page 29, for example, is a Grandmother's Flower Garden block; there are also Grandmother's Fan, Grandmother's Basket, and Grandmother's Engagement Ring, to mention just a few. I chose Duck and Ducklings for "Mother's Day," a Schoolhouse block for the "First Day of School," and Mexican Star for "Cinco de Mayo." There are many possibilities for other holidays. How about Pickle Dish for International Pickle Week, or a Drunkard's Path for the anniversary of the repeal of prohibition?

You can work this idea backwards by perusing the index of one of the excellent encyclopedias of quilt patterns. A single block, with or without a border, can make a 12" quilt. There are many blocks named for presidents, states, and cities. There are blocks called County Fair, May Basket, and Autumn Leaf. Make a Turkey Tracks block for Thanksgiving. Make a little Irish Chain quilt for St. Patrick's Day.

Sometimes, a particular type of fabric can represent the holiday, such as denim and plaid shirting for Labor Day. And what would be appropriate for Lawrence Welk's birthday? Polka dots, of course!

Novelty Fabrics

Some of my favorite quilts in this book are made primarily from novelty prints, also called conversation prints. These are fabrics printed with identifiable objects: rabbits, golf clubs, lobsters, teacups, and so on, practically *ad infinitum.* Never before have quilters had so many prints to choose from, and increasingly, they are available in 100% cotton. Novelty prints are great fun to use in quilts, and I enjoy shopping for them. If you have not worked much with novelty fabrics, make a

12" birthday quilt for a favorite aunt with novelty prints representing her hobbies, and I promise you, the floodgates will open. Suddenly, everywhere you will see fabrics that remind you of people and holidays you love. You will start collecting frog fabrics and dog fabrics and baseball fabrics. There will be wonderful surprises waiting for you in every fabric store you visit.

You can use novelty prints in traditional pieced or appliquéd designs, either as the dominant fabric in the quilt or just scattered among the other fabrics in a scrap quilt. Some of the quilts in this book, such as the Boss's Day quilt (page 29), are made almost entirely of individual motifs cut from novelty fabrics. These quilts are similar to collages, with no overall block design.

The "Mother's Day" quilt on page 25 is an example of using novelty prints in a traditional design. I chose the pattern Duck and Ducklings and made four blocks: one for each of my mother's three children, and a fourth for the only grandchild. I used different novelty prints that reflect our hobbies in each of the four blocks. The grandchild's block, for example, contains fabrics printed with athletic equipment, cats, jigsaw puzzle pieces, and her favorite cartoon character, Donald Duck. Even the white-on-muslin background fabrics, a different one for each block, reflect our interests. In this case, the block pattern used also reflected the theme of the quilt, but this is not necessary. For the opening day of baseball season, for example, you could make any block—a Churn Dash, perhaps—out of baseball fabrics.

The quilts made entirely from novelty fabrics are more unusual. The fabrics are cut in squares and rectangles of different sizes. These quilts take a little more time to plan so that everything fits together, but they allow you to use prints that are too large for the templates of most pieced blocks. The "Year of the Rabbit" quilt on page 95, for example, has rabbits that range in size from 1" to 5". Nonquilters find these novelty-print quilts especially charming; they make fun and unique gifts.

The Chinese New Year Cycle

The Chinese calendar, which has been in use for almost 4,000 years, is based on the phases of the moon. Each year is named after one of twelve animals in a repeating cycle. Some believe that people born under the sign of an animal will have personality traits associated with that animal. With the variety of novelty prints available today, you can make a quilt for almost any of these animals. You could add the characteristics as well—written, stenciled, embroidered, or quilted on the front of the quilt or on a label on the back.

Extend the calendar into the future or the past by adding or subtracting increments of twelve.

Year of the Rat
1936, 1948, 1960, 1972, 1984, 1996
*clever, honest, ambitious,
charming, gossipy*

Year of the Cow (Ox)
1937, 1949, 1961, 1973, 1985, 1997
*patient, hardworking, thoughtful,
persistent, dependable, honest*

Year of the Tiger
1938,1950, 1962, 1974, 1986, 1998
*courageous, powerful, impetuous,
successful, loyal, adventurous*

Year of the Rabbit
1939, 1951, 1963, 1975, 1987, 1999
*caring, grateful, talented, gossipy,
content, happy in a large family*

Year of the Dragon
1940, 1952, 1964, 1976, 1988, 2000
*powerful, energetic, independent,
flamboyant, imaginative*

Year of the Snake
1941, 1953, 1965, 1977, 1989, 2001
*crafty, wise, calm, elegant, good at
many things, subtle, sensuous*

Year of the Horse
1942, 1954, 1966, 1978, 1990, 2002
*strong, cheerful, friendly,
stylish, independent*

Year of the Sheep
1943, 1955, 1967, 1979, 1991, 2003
*affectionate, gentle, artistic, proud,
helpful, selfless*

Year of the Monkey
1944, 1956, 1968, 1980, 1992, 2004
*quick-witted, curious, versatile,
mischievous, a good parent*

Year of the Chicken
1945, 1957, 1969, 1981, 1993, 2005
*hardworking, careful, proud, confident,
independent, resolute*

Year of the Dog
1946,1958, 1970, 1982, 1994, 2006
*loyal, honest, reliable, likable,
generous, sympathetic*

Year of the Pig (Boar)
1947, 1959, 1971, 1983, 1995, 2007
*intelligent, generous, jolly, industrious,
noble, trusting, helpful*

General Instructions

Fabric Selection

In general, use 100% cotton fabrics for your quilts. Blends are more difficult to work with: they are slippery, they are often not as tightly woven so they warp out of shape, and they do not press with a sharp crease. If you mix blends and 100% cottons, the cottons will fade faster than the blends; as the quilt mellows, the blends will look harsh.

With the quilts in this book, however, I relaxed my rules a little. I would not use three yards of a blend in a bed quilt, but I used blends here and there in these little holiday quilts. Sometimes you may be forced to use blends. While you may not have trouble finding rabbit prints for a "Year of the Rabbit" quilt, you will have to be less fussy if you are looking for prints to celebrate the Year of the Snake. You may want to use odd fabrics specifically for their sheen or their fuzziness. Just be aware that they are often more difficult to tame than 100% cottons, and be careful when you press them: some fibers melt at the temperatures used to press cottons.

Rotary Cutting

You can prepare simple shapes for piecing much faster and more accurately by rotary cutting than by drawing around templates. In this book, cutting dimensions are provided for all squares, rectangles, and triangles; piecing templates are provided only for odd-shaped pieces, such as the spokes of the fans in the "April Showers" quilt.

You will need at least three pieces of equipment: a rotary cutter, a cutting mat designed for rotary cutters, and one or two transparent acrylic rulers. Do not try to use a rotary cutter without the special mat; you will quickly ruin the cutter blade. Ideally, you should have a mat that measures 24" in at least one dimension and a 24" x 6" ruler. A second ruler is not necessary if your mat has a 1" grid drawn on it, but a 12" ruler or a 6" Bias Square® is handy.

1. Press your fabric before cutting. Fold it with selvages together and lay it on the cutting mat with the fold toward you.
2. If you do not have a second ruler, place the folded edge on one of the grid lines on the mat. Then line up your long ruler with a vertical grid line so that the ruler just covers the raw edges of the fabric.

   If you have a second ruler, place it close to the left edge of the fabric and align the edge of the ruler with the fold. Lay the long ruler next to the short ruler so that it just covers the raw edges of the fabric, then remove the short ruler.

   Now cut the fabric with the rotary cutter, rolling the blade away from you, along the side of the long ruler.

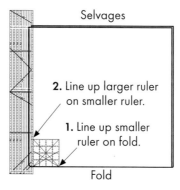

This first cut is called a clean-up cut. It tidies the edge of your fabric and ensures that the next cut will be exactly perpendicular to the fold. If the cuts are not perpendicular to the fold, the strips will have a dogleg instead of being perfectly straight when you open them up. Recheck the angle of your ruler after every two or three cuts and make another clean-up cut whenever necessary.

3. After you have tidied up the edge of the fabric, you are ready to cut the pieces for your quilt. Align the required measurement on the ruler with the newly cut edge of the fabric. Cut strips across the width of the fabric, from selvage to selvage, in the required width.

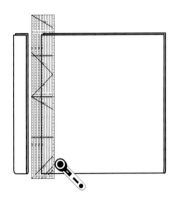

To cut squares:

Cut strips in the required widths. Trim away the selvage ends and crosscut the strips into pieces of the desired size. For example, if your design calls for 6 squares, each 4" x 4", cut a 4" strip across the width of the fabric, trim off the selvages, then make 3 crosscuts, each 4" wide.

To cut half-square triangles:

Cut a square ⅞" larger than the finished short side of the required triangle, to allow for seam allowances. Cut the square once diagonally. The short sides of a half-square triangle should be on the straight grain of the fabric.

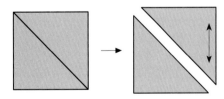

The icon "◫" is used to indicate that a square needs to be cut once diagonally to yield the required triangles

Machine Piecing

Maintaining an exact ¼" seam is most important in machine piecing. If you do not sew accurate ¼" seams, the lines of the designs won't match up, the points of your triangles won't be pointed, the blocks won't fit together properly, and the whole piece won't lie flat.

On many sewing machines, the edge of the presser foot is exactly ¼" from the needle. On some machines, the needle position is movable. On other machines, you will need to make a ¼" seam guide by placing a piece of masking tape on the throat plate.

Test the accuracy of your ¼" seams by sewing a pieced block and measuring it. Even if you appear to be making accurate ¼" seams, your block may be a little too small. This happens because a little of the fabric is taken up by the bump where each seam allowance is pressed. Most quilters find they need to take a seam allowance that is just a thread or two under ¼". Practice making slight alterations in your seam width until your blocks are consistently the right size.

Pressing

Careful and thorough pressing is one of the most important and often neglected aspects of quiltmaking. There are two basic rules of pressing when you machine sew:

1. Press all seam allowances to one side.

Seam allowances are pressed to one side for strength; when seam allowances are pressed open, the stitching of the seam is exposed and more subject to wear.

Pressing the seam allowances to one side also allows you to press matching seams in opposite directions; you can then butt seams against each another and more easily match seam lines. In this book, arrows are provided to indicate the direction to press seam allowances at almost every step. When you have to match seam lines several steps later, the seam allowances will already be pressed in opposite directions.

When it is not necessary to match seams, the pressing arrows indicate the direction that will reduce bulk. When bulk is not an issue, press toward the darker fabric.

2. *Press each seam before crossing it with another seam.*

If you do not press a seam flat before you cross it with another seam, a little tuck will form where the seam allowance is folded to one side. Once you cross that tuck with another seam, the tuck is caught in the stitching and becomes permanent; no amount of pressing will flatten it. These little tucks will make your block smaller than it should be. Discipline your-self to press your seams before proceeding to the next step. From the front of the piece, push the broad side of the iron sideways into the bump of the seam and flatten it.

Speed Piecing

Speed piecing is a combination of rotary cutting and shortcut sewing techniques. Many speed-pieced designs require a strip unit, which is made by sewing fabric strips to-gether lengthwise. The strip unit is pressed and crosscut into segments. The segments are then sewn together to make a design.

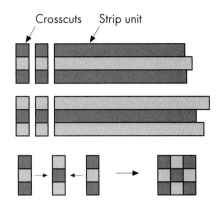

Crosscuts   Strip unit

1. Sew the strips together carefully, with exact ¼" seams, so all the finished strip widths are equal. The unit must also be straight; if the bottom fabric feeds into the sewing machine faster than the top fabric or vice versa, the unit will curve. To combat this tendency, sew pairs of strips together top to bottom, then sew the pairs to each other bottom to top.

2. Press the strip unit carefully so that it lies perfectly flat, with no pleats at the seams. The pattern instructions will tell you which direction to press the seam allowances. Press the wrong side first, then flip the unit over and press the right side, pushing the broad side of the iron into the bump at each seam, flattening it.

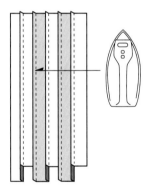

If the unit curves just slightly, you may be able to steam it back into line. If not, make frequent clean-up cuts as you cross-cut. The crosscuts must be perpendicular to the seam lines, or your little squares will not be square.

Foundation Piecing

Foundation piecing is a popular technique in which fabric pieces are sewn, one by one, to a design drawn on a paper or muslin foundation. All seams are sewn directly on the drawn lines, through the foundation. The beauty of foundation piecing is that you can piece very complicated designs with absolutely no templates. The technique is also useful for miniature blocks, where it can be difficult to sew together tiny pieces with accuracy. When you sew the designs on foundation paper, the lines and points of the design are always neat and clean.

If you are new to foundation piecing, try a variety of foundation materials until you find one you like.

- Tracing paper is my favorite, because you can see through it; the drawn design is visible on both sides. You cannot photocopy onto tracing paper, however, so you must trace each line by hand. A good inexpensive substitute for tracing paper is examination-table paper. Next time you are in for a checkup, ask the nurse if she will roll off a yard or two for you.
- Regular paper (typing paper) is a little more difficult to remove after piecing. You must hold the piece up to the light to see through it, but you can quickly make a number of photocopies of your design.
- Muslin does not have to be removed, but you cannot see through it easily, and I think it wiggles too much; I like the rigidity of paper for greater piecing accuracy.

To foundation piece:

1. Trace the design accurately on a paper or muslin foundation. Draw a ¼"-wide seam allowance beyond the outer edges of the design. Copy the numbers as well; they indicate the order in which to sew the pieces. Scribble a little shading or mark with an X the shaded areas of the design, to indicate which fabric to use for each section. Cut the paper or muslin foundation a bit larger than the design.

2. Cut a piece of fabric roughly the shape of piece #1 in the design, adding about ¼" for a seam allowance. Put it on the wrong side of the foundation, right side up.

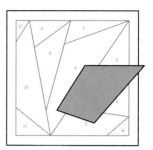

3. Cut a piece of fabric roughly the shape of piece #2 plus seam allowance. Pin it to fabric piece #1, right sides together. Check that both pieces overlap the seam line by at least ⅛".

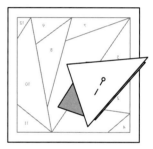

4. Turn the unit over so the printed side of the foundation is up and the fabric is on the underside. Sew the seam exactly on the drawn line, extending the seam ¼" beyond the drawn line on both ends. Do not backstitch at either end.

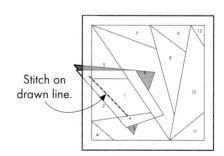

Stitch on drawn line.

5. Trim the seam allowances to ¼".
6. Turn the unit so the fabric is on top again. Flip fabric piece #2 open so it is right side up. Press with a dry iron.

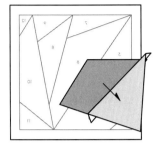

7. Add piece #3 in the same manner: pin it in place on the wrong side of the foundation, turn the unit over, and sew the seam on the drawn line. Turn the unit back over, trim the seam allowances, flip fabric piece #3 open, and press.
8. Add the remaining pieces in order, then trim the edges of the block, leaving a ¼"-wide seam allowance beyond the outer lines of the marked design. Use the outer lines for guidance, but use measurements on the rotary ruler to cut the block to the exact size needed (including ¼"-wide seam allowances).
9. If you used a paper foundation, remove it now, working from the outside edges to the center of the design.

Note: Many foundation designs are assembled in several units, which are then sewn together. Do not remove the foundation paper on these designs until they are completely assembled. In fact, you may prefer to leave the foundation paper in until after the blocks are sewn together, because the outer edges of many foundation-pieced blocks are on the bias. If you leave the foundation paper in, the bias edges will not stretch out of shape.

Reversing Designs

To reverse a foundation design, photocopy it and tape the photocopy to a window, wrong side toward you, so that you can see the design through the paper. Draw the reversed design on the wrong side of the paper. Use this as your design for tracing or photocopying.

Enlarging Designs

Unlike templates with seam allowances, foundation-pieced designs are easily enlarged with a photocopier. Take the foundation pattern to a photocopy shop and ask to have it enlarged. For example, if you start with the 3" leaf block on page 117, a 200% enlargement will make a 6" block. Two or more copies may be required if the enlarged sections will not fit on one page.

Photocopiers often distort the image slightly. To compensate, extend the outer pieces of fabric a little more than ¼" beyond the outside edges of the block. Then trim the completed block to the exact size needed (including ¼"-wide seam allowances). The extra fabric will help if the enlargement is slightly distorted.

String Piecing

String piecing is a very old foundation-piecing technique. Our great-grandmothers used string piecing to make fabric out of otherwise useless scraps. Start with a paper or muslin foundation. Cover the foundation with narrow strips of fabric from one end to the other: sew, flip, and press; sew, flip, and press. Use the resulting piece of fabric just as you would any other piece of fabric. Trim it to the desired size with your rotary cutter, or paper-patch it for appliqué.

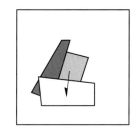

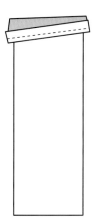

Spiral Crazy Patchwork

This technique is similar to string piecing. Instead of working from one end of a foundation to the other, start in the center. Then add fabrics either clockwise or counterclockwise to build the fabric from the center out in a spiral. Sew, flip, and press; sew, flip, and press. Again, you can trim the resulting fabric to size or paper-patch it for appliqué.

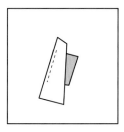
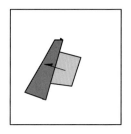

Appliqué

Paper-Patch Appliqué

I recommend the appliqué method called paper patch. Each piece takes a little time to prepare, but even beginners can quickly achieve smooth curves and precise shapes.

The appliqué templates do not include seam allowances.

1. Trace the template onto plastic template material and cut out carefully, then trace around it onto lightweight card stock or construction paper. Cut out the paper piece very carefully, making any curves as smooth as possible. Refer to the illustration of the quilt and mark the right side of each paper piece.

2. Lay the paper piece on the wrong side of your fabric, right side down. Pin it in place. Cut out the fabric, adding a ¼"-wide seam allowance all around the paper piece.

3. Fold the seam allowance under and baste it in place, sewing through the paper piece. Pull the seam allowance smoothly over curves. When you have basted all

around, the fabric should be quite taut over the paper piece.

Clip around inside curves almost to the paper piece. Make the clips at least ¼" apart or the fabric will fray. When you come to a corner, baste one edge down all the way to the corner, then fold the other edge over it and continue basting.

4. After you have basted the paper patch, press it thoroughly. Leave the paper and the basting stitches in.

5. Appliqué the piece to the background fabric with an almost invisible stitch. Use thread that matches the appliqué piece, not the background fabric. Secure the knot on the wrong side of the background fabric. Catch just a few threads at the edge of the piece. Send the needle down directly under the place where you caught the edge of the piece. Bring the needle up ⅛" to ¼" away from the previous stitch and again catch just a few threads at the edge of the piece. Only a tiny stitch should show on the front of the quilt; all the traveling is done on the wrong side.

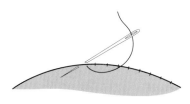

Appliqué stitch

6. Stitch almost all the way around the paper patch, leaving 1" to 2" unstitched. Remove the basting threads and then reach in with a pair of tweezers and pull out the paper. After you have removed all the paper, finish appliquéing the piece.

If the piece is very small or has a shape that makes removing the paper difficult, sew the piece completely down and remove the paper through one or more slits in the background fabric under the patch. It is not necessary to sew up the slits; the stitching around the patches will stabilize the area.

Transferring Appliqué Designs

To transfer a large appliqué design to your background fabric, locate the center of the background square by folding it in half diagonally and lightly finger-pressing a crease at the center.

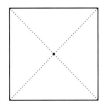

The centers of the appliqué designs in this book are marked with a dot. Place the center of the background fabric over the center dot of the design and lightly mark the positions of each appliqué piece. If you cannot see the design through your background fabric, photocopy the design and tape it to a window. Tape your background fabric over the design and lightly trace.

Fusible Appliqué

If you do not want to spend the time required for traditional appliqué, you might want to try fusing your appliqué designs. With this technique, you "cut and paste" the fabric pieces to the background, eliminating all sewing. You don't even have to turn under the edges of the fabric pieces. This is a good technique for designs that are difficult to do in traditional appliqué, such as designs with very small pieces or sharp points. Note that this technique always reverses your design; the final product will be the mirror image of the original design.

Fusible appliqué requires a paper-backed fusible web. Many brands and weights are available, including Wonder-Under® and HeatnBond®. Lightweight web is used to hold the piece temporarily while it is machine- or hand-stitched in place. Heavyweight web is used to hold the piece in place permanently without any stitching.

Always practice first with scraps of your fabric. Test each brand of fusible web and each type of fabric you plan to use.

To fuse an appliqué piece:
1. Draw the design, reversed, on the paper side of the fusible web.
2. Cut out the design, adding a little extra around all edges.
3. Place the design, fusible web side down, on the wrong side of fabric. Press in place with a warm iron. Follow the directions on the package for the temperature of the iron and the length of time to press.
4. Cut out the design on the drawn line.
5. Peel the paper off the back.
6. Lay the design on background fabric, fusible web side down. Press in place.

UltraSuede® Appliqué

UltraSuede is a wonderful fabric to use for appliqué because it is not necessary to turn under the edges. This makes it a good choice for designs with small pieces or sharp points. It is also washable.

Because pins and needles make permanent holes in UltraSuede, it is necessary to hold the pieces in place by fusing them, rather than pinning or basting them.

Basting the Quilt

For the 12" square quilts, cut the backing fabric 13" x 13". Be sure you do not include any selvages, which can draw in the edges and prevent the backing from lying flat.

The batting used for most of the quilts in this book was Pellon®. It works especially well for small wall hangings because it is very stable and does not have to be closely quilted. It is thin, which is good for a small piece, and slightly stiff, which is good for a piece that will hang on a wall. Cut a 13" square of batting for each quilt.

Lay the pressed quilt backing on a table, wrong side up. Lay the batting on top of the quilt backing. Center the quilt top over the batting. If you plan to hand quilt, baste the layers together with 1" stitches, in horizontal and vertical lines about 2" apart. Always baste with white thread; colored thread may leave little colored dots when you remove it after quilting. Also baste all around the quilt about ¼" in from the edges; this will hold the edges together when you add the binding later.

If you plan to machine quilt, pin the layers together with straight pins or safety pins. Pin around the edges to hold them together for binding later.

Quilting

Quilting is the stitching that holds together the back, batting, and quilt top. You can quilt by hand or by machine.

Hand Quilting

1. Place the basted quilt in a hoop or quilting frame. For these small quilts, an 11" square plastic frame works well. Start in the center of the quilt and quilt in sections toward the edges, moving the hoop as necessary. Use short quilting needles called Betweens, and the heavy thread sold as hand-quilting thread. You will also need a quilting thimble, which is like a regular thimble except that it has an indentation on the end rather than a rounded end.
2. Tie a small knot in the end of the thread. With the needle, wiggle a hole in the surface of the quilt about ½" from where you plan to start quilting. Push the threaded

needle in through the hole and back out on top of the quilt where you plan to start, pulling the knot through the hole to bury it in the batting. There should be no knots showing on either the top or the bottom of the quilt.

3. Quilt with a running stitch. Use the quilting thimble on your third finger to push the needle through the quilt, rocking the needle up and down to help make the stitches smaller.

4. When you reach the end of your thread or a stopping place in your design, tie a knot in the thread. Pull the knot into the batting and cut the thread even with the surface of the quilt.

Be sure stitches go through all three layers.

Machine Quilting

Machine quilt with regular sewing thread or with the thin nylon thread made for machine quilting. If you use nylon thread, use regular thread in the bobbin. Set the machine for a stitch slightly longer than what you use for regular sewing. Whenever possible, start and stop your quilting at the edges of the quilt and backstitch for security. The binding will cover the ends. When you must start and stop in the middle of the quilt, leave 4" thread ends. When you are finished, thread each end on a needle, pull it inside the quilt through the batting, and trim near the quilt surface.

Binding

All the quilts in this book are finished with a ½" straight-grain, double-fold binding.

1. Cut strips from the binding fabric 2¾" wide. Two 44" strips will be enough to go around the quilt, with enough extra for joining the strips and turning corners.

2. Join the strips at right angles with a diago-

nal seam. Trim away excess fabric, leaving a ¼"-wide seam allowance. Press the seams open.

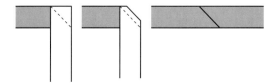

3. Trim one end to a 45° angle and press under ¼". Fold the strip in half lengthwise, wrong sides together, and press.

4. Trim the quilt so that the batting and backing extend ¼" beyond the raw edge of the quilt top.

5. With right sides together, match the raw edges of the binding with the edges of the quilt top (not the edges of the batting and backing) and take a ¼"-wide seam. Start with the end cut to a 45° angle and end by overlapping the angled end with the binding strip. Stop the seam at each corner, ¼" from the edge of the quilt top, and backstitch.

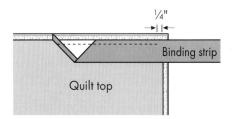

6. At the corner, fold the binding strip away from you and then back toward you as shown. Line up the fold with the edges of the batting and backing, and the raw edges of the binding strip with the edge of the quilt top. Start sewing the next side at the edge of the fold; backstitch. Repeat at each corner.

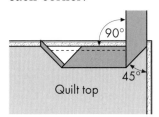
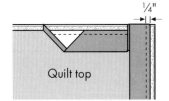

7. Fold the binding to the back of the quilt and blindstitch in place. At each corner, a miter will form automatically on the front of the quilt; fold the binding to make a miter on the back.

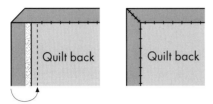

Straight-Corner Binding

If you do not want to miter the corners, you can apply a straight-corner binding. Sew the binding strip to the quilt along the top and bottom edges, matching the raw edges of the binding strip to the edge of the quilt top and taking a ¼"-wide seam. Trim the binding even with the batting and backing at each end. Fold the binding to the back of the quilt and blindstitch in place. Then sew the binding to the sides of the quilt, turning under ¼" at each end. Blindstitch the ends closed.

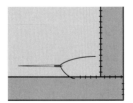

Embellishments

Embroidery

You can embroider details with the simple stitches shown here.

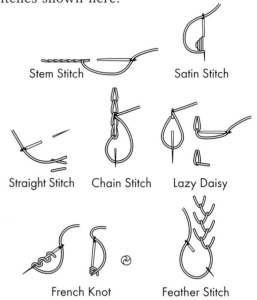

Fabric Paint

Dimensional fabric paint is available at most fabric and variety stores in small plastic squeeze bottles. It is intended for painting T-shirts and sweatshirts, and is thick and glossy when it dries. Always practice first before painting on your quilt. The metallic paints in particular may look quite different when dry than they do when first applied. You can substitute fabric paint for embroidery details and paint eyes and noses instead of sewing on beads.

Stenciling

Stenciling requires stencil paint and a purchased or handmade cardboard or plastic stencil. You can make your own stencils from template plastic or lightweight cardboard. Plastic is best for a stencil you plan to reuse, since the water-soluble stencil paint will wash off easily. Draw the design on the template material and cut out the stencil with an X-Acto™ knife or small, sharp scissors.

Apply the stencil paint with a slightly damp sponge or a stencil brush. The brush part of a stencil brush is round and 1" to 2" in diameter. Tape the bristles together into a solid circle by winding a piece of masking tape around them.

Tape the stencil to your fabric. With the sponge or taped stencil brush, pick up a small amount of paint and dab it on the fabric. Dab forcefully with the sponge, or pound the brush up and down to force the paint into the fabric. Work carefully around the edges of the design; press down firmly on the stencil with the fingers of one hand as you apply paint with the other to prevent the paint from seeping under the edges of the stencil. To make the design appear three-dimensional, paint thoroughly around the edges and lightly in the center.

Beading

Beads are available in a wide range of colors and sizes. Plastic beads are inexpensive; glass beads are luxurious. You will need a beading needle, available at most fabric stores, and nylon thread. Beading a quilt is usually the final step. Otherwise, the beads may get in the way of your hoop if you hand quilt, or the presser foot if you machine quilt or when you attach the binding.

For single isolated beads, take a stitch through the bead, then take another stitch through the bead to anchor it in place. Fasten off the thread.

For a group of beads, either take a single stitch through each bead or couch down a strand of beads. To couch, bring the thread up through the quilt, string the beads on it, and take the thread down through the quilt. Then go back and take a tiny stitch between each bead or between every two or three beads, anchoring the strand.

Spray Glitter

Spray glitter is the pixie dust of the 1990s. It is one of those things you didn't know you needed, but once you have it, you find many uses for it. It lends instant glamour and sparkle to any quilt. It is especially nice for quilts that celebrate the more festive holidays: Christmas, New Year's, and birthdays, for example.

Spray glitter is available in small aerosol cans at most craft supply stores. Spray it lightly on your finished quilt. The first time you glitter is a big step, but I have been happy with the results every time I have used it. Some of the glitter will pop off the surface of the quilt as it is handled. Store your glittered quilts away from your other quilts. I store each of my 12" glittered quilts in a 13" x 13" zipper-seal plastic bag.

The glitter will come off in the washing machine, so the decision to glitter is reversible if the quilt is washable.

The Quilts

The rest of the book is devoted to directions for the 12" square quilts illustrated in the color gallery on pages 21–32 . The dates of the holidays these quilts were meant to celebrate are listed in the table of contents. Many of the quilts are appropriate for several holidays; examples of other possibilities are often given in the introductions to the designs. Some of the designs may be appropriate to celebrate family birthdays or events. A number of the designs are seasonal rather than based on a specific holiday, so you can have quilts to display between holidays and family celebrations.

All the directions in this section are for 12" square quilts. Some of them are actually miniature quilts, assembled from 3" or 4" blocks. Some, such as "Eliza Doolittle Day" and "Holly Wreath," are made from one 12" block. Many different quiltmaking and embellishing techniques were employed, some just to spark your imagination. For example, only one quilt is stenciled, but stenciled messages and embellishments could be added to any of the others.

There are quilts for every skill level, from beginner to experienced. The simple pieced quilts for Flag Day, Presidents' Day, and Mother's Day are easy enough to be your first rotary-cutting project. Some of the appliqué designs offer a challenge, although all are simple to do in fusible appliqué. Collage quilts, such as "Boss's Day," feature novelty prints and are fun for both the novice and the experienced quilter: the novice, because they are easy to assemble, and the experienced quilter, because at last she can demonstrate why she needs twenty-seven bunny fabrics.

The cutting charts contain directions for cutting individual pieces from specific fabrics. Directions for cutting pieces that require foundation-piecing techniques are included in the assembly steps. Numbers preceded by a "T" indicate paper-patch templates. These are located on pages 97–123.

If you are new to foundation piecing, "Falling Leaves" and "Adopt-a-Shelter-Cat Month" are easy designs for learning the technique. If you are already a devotee of foundation piecing, the graceful trotting horse of "Kentucky Derby Day" will test your expertise.

Chinese New Year by Janet Kime, 1994, ▶
Vashon Island, Washington, 12" x 12".
Glittering with gold, this red and black
dragon is a symbol of the Chinese
New Year. Directions on page 33.

Martin Luther King, Jr. Day by Janet Kime, 1995, ▶
Vashon Island, Washington, 12" x 12". Celebrate
several holidays with special meaning to African-
Americans, including African-American History
Month (February), with a vivid quilt in bold African
colors. Directions on page 34.

◀ **Valentine's Day** by Janet Kime, 1995, Vashon Island,
Washington, 12" x 12". What could be more romantic
than hearts and flowers, lavishly embellished with lace,
embroidery, and pearls? Directions on page 36.

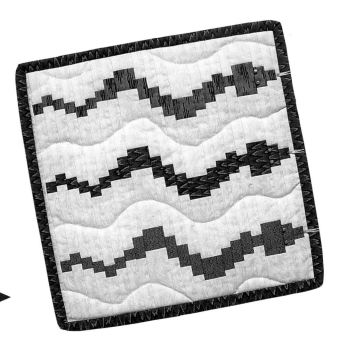

Presidents' Day by Janet Kime, 1994, Vashon Island, Washington, 11" x 11". Celebrate the births of Presidents Washington and Lincoln with a Lincoln's Platform block and cherries everywhere. Directions on page 38.

St. Patrick's Day by Joel T. Patz, 1995, Seattle, Washington, 12" x 12". The many feats credited to the Irish saint include driving all the snakes from Ireland. These three are green, of course. Directions on page 40.

Swallows' Return by Janet Kime, 1995, Vashon Island, Washington, 12" x 12". On March 19, each spring, cliff swallows return to nest in the mission of San Juan Capistrano in California. Directions on page 42.

Buzzards' Return by Janet Kime, 1995, Vashon Island, Washington, 12" x 12". San Juan Capistrano has nothing over Hinckley, Ohio; on March 15, each spring, the buzzards return to Hinckley. Directions on page 43.

Solstice/Equinox Quilt by Janet Kime, ➤
1995, Vashon Island, Washington,
12" x 12". Glittery appliquéd astrological
signs represent the summer and winter solstices and the spring and autumn equinoxes.
Directions on page 44.

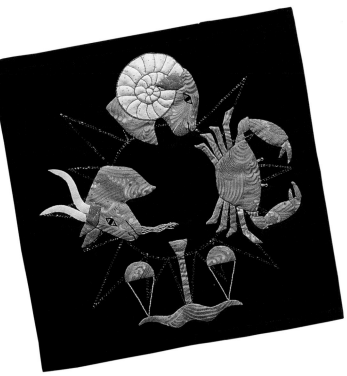

April Showers by Virginia Morrison, 1995,
Vashon Island, Washington, 12" x 12". Wel-
come spring with this pretty pastel quilt.
Directions on page 46.

The Easter Tree by Janet Kime, 1995, Vashon ➤
Island, Washington, 12" x 12". Piece and
appliqué fancy eggs for a quilter's Easter tree.
Directions on page 47.

Trees 'n' Breeze by Joel T. Patz, 1995, ▶
Seattle, Washington, 12" x 12". White-on-
muslin paisley breezes swirl around these
strip-pieced trees, celebrating Arbor Day.
Directions on page 50.

Cinco de Mayo by Janet Kime, 1995, Vashon
Island, Washington, 12" x 12". Four Mexican
Star blocks in Southwest colors celebrate the
Mexican victory over the French in 1862.
Directions on page 52. ▼

Eliza Doolittle Day by Janet Kime, 1995, ▶
Vashon Island, Washington, 12" x 12".
The 20th of May is Eliza Doolittle Day—at
least according to the musical "My Fair Lady."
Directions on page 58.

Kentucky Derby Day by Janet Kime, 1995, ▶
Vashon Island, Washington, 12" x 12". A
proud foundation-pieced horse, ready for
the Run for the Roses. Directions on page 54.

Be Kind to Animals by Janet Kime, 1995, Vashon Island, Washington, 12" x 12". Foundation-pieced bunnies, Siamese cats, a dog, frogs, fish, even an appliquéd snake—what could be easier to love? Directions on page 55.

Mother's Day by Janet Kime, 1995, Vashon Island, Washington, 12" x 12". Four Duck and Ducklings blocks—one for each child and grandchild—make up this special wall hanging for the quilter's mother. Directions on page 56. ▼

Adopt-a-Shelter-Cat Month by Marilyn Bacon, ▶ 1995, Edmonds, Washington, 12" x 12". These lovable cats in pretty pastels are looking for a home. Directions on page 59.

Flag Day by Janet Kime, 1995, Vashon Island, Washington, 12" x 12". Four U.S. flags whirl around in this red, white, and blue patriotic quilt. Directions on page 60.

Father's Day by Janet Kime, 1995, Vashon Island, Washington, 12" x 12". One of the reasons God gave daddies patience is so they could teach us to fish. Directions on page 61.

Independence Day by Karen Gabriel and Janet Kime, 1995, Princeton Junction, New Jersey, 12" x 12". Spangly fireworks explode on this patriotic quilt. Directions on page 63.

◀ **Bastille Day** by Janet Kime, 1994, Vashon Island, Washington, 12" x 12". Celebrate the beginning of the French Revolution with a Bargello design in the colors of the French flag. Directions on page 65.

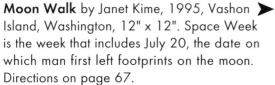

Moon Walk by Janet Kime, 1995, Vashon ▶ Island, Washington, 12" x 12". Space Week is the week that includes July 20, the date on which man first left footprints on the moon. Directions on page 67.

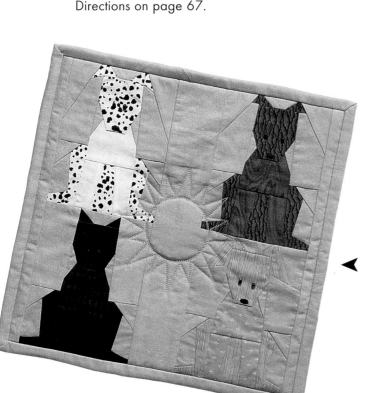

◀ **Dog Days of Summer** by Virginia Morrison and Janet Kime, 1995, Seattle, Washington, 12" x 12". Four foundation-pieced bowsers pant in the summer sun. Directions on page 68.

County Fair by Virginia Morrison, 1995, Seattle, Washington, 12" x 12". There are so many sights to see at a county fair: prize vegetables, animals, and, of course, quilts. Directions on page 70.

Ballooning by Janet Kime, 1995, Vashon Island, Washington, 12" x 12". Celebrate summer with bright hot-air balloons drifting across the sky. Directions on page 72.

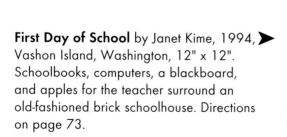

Boss's Day by Janet Kime, 1995, Vashon Island, Washington, 12" x 12". This quilt is for anyone who has ever had an oinker for a boss! Directions on page 78.

First Day of School by Janet Kime, 1994, Vashon Island, Washington, 12" x 12". Schoolbooks, computers, a blackboard, and apples for the teacher surround an old-fashioned brick schoolhouse. Directions on page 73.

◀ **Grandparents' Day** by Janet Kime, 1994, Vashon Island, Washington, 12" x 12". Remember your grandparents with an English paper-pieced Grandmother's Flower Garden block. Directions on page 75.

▲

Falling Leaves by Janet Kime, 1994, Vashon Island, Washington, 12" x 12". Leaves in bright autumn colors tumble down to earth in a quilt celebrating the end of summer. Directions on page 76.

Columbus Day by Janet Kime, 1994, Vashon ▶ Island, Washington, 12" x 12". The Niña, Pinta, and Santa María braved the seas to discover the Americas in 1492. Directions on page 77.

Happy Halloween by Janet Kime, 1994, Vashon Island, Washington, 12" x 12". Big black spiders lurk around this quilt to celebrate all-spooks day. Directions on page 80.

Thanksgiving by Janet Kime, 1994, Vashon Island, Washington, 12" x 12". Harvest fruits and vegetables spill over this quilt celebrating America's bounty. Directions on page 83.

Hanukkah by Janet Kime, 1994, Vashon Island, Washington, 12" x 12". The menorah, an eight-branched candelabrum with a ninth candle used to light the others, is a symbol of the Jewish Festival of Lights. Directions on page 84.

St. Lucia Day by Janet Kime, 1994, Vashon ▶ Island, Washington, 12" x 12". An appliquéd and embroidered Lucia crown in Swedish colors represents this traditional Scandinavian Christmas-season holiday. Directions on page 86.

◀ **Veterans Day** by Janet Kime, 1994, Vashon Island, Washington, 12" x 12". Traditionally, blue stars represent family members who served in wartime, and gold stars represent those who gave their lives. Directions on page 82.

◀ **Holly Wreath** by Janet Kime, 1994, Vashon Island, Washington, 12" x 12". Holly leaves and a big bow are fused to the background fabric and then covered with a shimmery layer of organdy. Directions on page 87.

Snow Flurries by Karen Gabriel, 1995, Princeton ▶ Junction, New Jersey, 12" x 12". Snowflakes— crocheted, appliquéd, quilted, beaded, and sequined—are scattered against a night sky. Directions on page 88.

Checkered Border Quilt by Virginia Morrison, 1995, Seattle, Washington, 18" x 18". Want a quilt a little larger than 12" square? Make an easy Checkered Border quilt and attach a quilt to the center, changing the quilt with each holiday. Directions on page 89. ▼

▲ **Accordian-Pleat Border Quilt** by Janet Kime, 1995, Vashon Island, Washington, 24½" x 24½". Speed-piece this border quilt with four solid or tone-on-tone fabrics and a background fabric. Directions on page 90.

Quilt

Chinese New Year

Color photo on page 21

Chinese New Year begins the evening of the second new moon following the winter solstice. The fifteen-day celebration culminates with the Parade of Lanterns through the streets, led by a huge paper dragon. Asian dragons, unlike western dragons, are friendly and helpful. In the New Year celebration, they represent goodness and strength. Chinese New Year begins on February 19 in 1996, and February 8 in 1997. You can also use this quilt to celebrate the birthday of anyone born in a Year of the Dragon (see page 8).

Look for red fabrics with metallic gold highlights for your dragon, then paint his tendrils, teeth, and claws with gold fabric paint and add spray glitter for even more sparkle.

Materials: 44"-wide fabric

Assorted scraps of red prints with metallic gold for dragon
²⁄₃ yd. for background (includes backing and binding)
13" square of batting
Black embroidery floss
6mm black bead
Metallic gold fabric paint
Gold spray glitter (optional)

Cutting

Fabric	Piece No.	No. of Pieces	Dimensions
Red print	T3	2 + 1r	
Background		1	12½" x 12½"

Assembly

Refer to String Piecing and Paper-Patch Appliqué on page 14. Use templates on pages 97—98.

1. Transfer T1 and T2 to tracing paper for foundation piecing.

2. String-piece strips of red fabrics in random widths onto the paper foundations to make the dragon body and tail. Extend the ends ¼" as shown by the dotted lines on T1 and T2. Trim away excess fabric, leaving ¼" to turn under. Tear away the paper foundations.
3. Paper-patch the dragon body, tail, and 3 legs.
4. Appliqué the dragon body (T1) to the background square, tucking the raw edge under the body and leaving a 2" opening where the tail (T2) emerges. Remove the paper from the body. Pin tail in place, tucking the raw edge under the dragon body. Appliqué the tail.
5. Appliqué the legs (T3) in place.

Finishing

Refer to pages 16–19 to finish your quilt.

1. Layer the quilt top with 13" squares of batting and backing. Trim the batting and backing so they extend ¼" beyond the quilt top. Baste.
2. Quilt around the dragon.
3. Bind the edges.
4. Embroider the nostril and outline of the eye. Attach a black bead for the eye.
5. Use metallic gold fabric paint to draw the tendrils, teeth, and claws. Let dry 24 hours.
6. Add spray glitter if desired.

Quilt

Martin Luther King, Jr. Day

Color photo on page 21

January 15 is the actual birthday of the Reverand Dr. Martin Luther King, Jr., but it is celebrated as a national holiday on the third Monday in January. February is designated African-American History Month because it is the month including the birthdays of Abraham Lincoln and Frederick Douglass. It is also the month the fifteenth Amendment to the Constitution was ratified, guaranteeing the right of citizens to vote regardless of race, color, or previous condition of servitude.

Other dates to celebrate with this quilt: January 1, the date of the Emancipation Proclamation in 1863; August 28, the date of the 1963 March on Washington and the "I Have a Dream" speech; December 18, the date of the ratification of the Thirteenth Amendment to the Constitution, abolishing slavery; the last week of December, Kwanzaa, an American celebration based on traditional African harvest festivals.

Imitate some of the African-American quilts made in the 1800s, using strong colors and fabrics printed with bold African designs.

Materials: 44"-wide fabric

⅛ yd. each of several African prints
⅛ yd. for background
⅛ yd. of red for star and lettering
13" square of batting
½ yd. for backing
¼ yd. for binding

Cutting

Note: Some of the pieces you cut may not look like the corresponding pieces in the block diagram because some of the diagonals are speed-pieced. The diagram shows you the location of each piece, not necessarily its actual shape.

Fabric	Piece No.	No. of Pieces	Dimensions
African prints	1	3	1½" x 12½"
Background	2	1	3½" x 12½"
	3	4	2" x 2"
	4	4	2" x 3½"
Red	3	8	2" x 2"

Assembly

Refer to Paper-Patch Appliqué and String Piecing on page 14. Use letter templates on page 98.

1. Paper-patch the letters and appliqué to background piece 2. Or, if you prefer, fuse the letters to the background instead.
2. To make the star-point units, speed-piece a red 3 to each end of a background 4. Make 4 units.

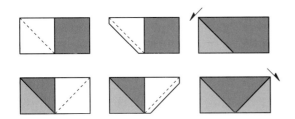

3. Cut an irregular square about 2½" x 2½" for the center of the star. Piece irregular strips to the 4 sides of the square. Trim the piece to 3½" x 3½".

4. Assemble the center, the star-point units, and the background squares 3 to make the star block.

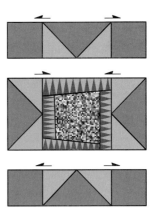

5. On foundation paper, draw 2 rectangles, each 3½" x 6½". String-piece each rectangle, using assorted African prints. Trim each to 3½" x 6½". Sew to opposite sides of the star block.

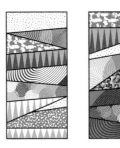

6. Sew the African print strips, the star unit, and the FREEDOM strip together to complete the quilt top.

Finishing

Refer to pages 16–19 to finish your quilt.

1. Layer the quilt top with 13" squares of batting and backing. Trim the batting and backing so they extend ¼" beyond the quilt top. Baste.
2. Quilt in-the-ditch of the horizontal strips 1 and around the star.
3. Bind the edges.

This is a great small project to experiment with Crazy quilting. The construction is traditional, even down to an embroidered spider web, but instead of the heavy blacks and velvets of the 1800s, update your quilt with lightweight fabrics in delicate pinks.

This quilt could also be displayed on the birthday of your spouse or sweetheart, on your wedding anniversary, or on any other romantic anniversary you celebrate together.

Materials: 44"-wide fabric

Assorted scraps of pinks
13" square of batting
½ yd. for backing
¼ yd. for binding
Embellishments (see Hint box on page 37)

Cutting

Fabric	Piece No.	No. of Pieces	Dimensions
Asst. pinks	T2	6	
	T3	1	
Light pink		1	7½" x 7½"
		1	5" x 5"

Assembly

Refer to Spiral Crazy Patchwork and Paper-Patch Appliqué on page 14. Use templates on page 99.

1. Draw the heart (T1) on foundation paper or muslin. Spiral crazy-piece the heart. Trim excess fabric, leaving a ¼"-wide seam allowance all around, and appliqué to a 7½" square of light pink fabric.

2. Sew 6 fan spokes (T2) together on the long edges to make the fan.

3. Baste under ¼" on the long curved edge and appliqué the fan to a 5" square of light pink fabric, tucking lace under the curved edge if desired. Paper-patch the fan base (T3) on the curved edge only and appliqué to the corner of the fan, again tucking lace under the curved edge if desired.

4. Cut a 12½" x 12½" square of foundation paper. This will be the final size of the block, including seam allowances.

5. Pin the fan square to the lower right corner of the foundation paper, matching the raw edges with the edges of the paper. Pin the heart square to the upper left corner of the foundation paper, about 1½" in from the top and left edges of the paper.

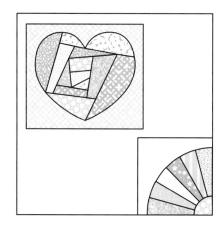

6. Add irregular pieces of pink fabrics around the heart as if the heart square were the center of a spiral crazy-patch piece. Cover the foundation paper.

Note: In some places, particularly when you meet the fan square, it will be necessary to leave some edges raw, or turn them under and machine-stitch them down. These edges can be covered later with lace, ribbon, or embroidery. Strips of lace and ribbon can also be added as you crazy-piece; cover the cut ends as you add the next pieces of fabric.

7. Press the completed square carefully. Staystitch all around the outer edge, ⅛" in from the edge of the foundation paper. Trim excess fabric around the edges of the paper. Remove the paper.
8. Use silver metallic thread to embroider the spider web and spider in the upper right corner (see pattern below). Add lace, ribbon, and other embroidered embellishments. Add embellishments such as beads and brass charms after the piece has been quilted and bound so they don't interfere with the quilting frame or the presser foot as you sew on the binding.

Finishing

Refer to pages 16–19 to finish your quilt.
1. Layer the quilt top with 13" squares of batting and backing. Trim the batting and backing so they extend ¼" beyond the quilt top. Baste.
2. Quilt as desired.
3. Bind the edges.
4. Add any remaining embellishments.

Hint
Crazy-Quilt Embellishments

Embroidery floss
Metallic and rayon embroidery threads
Ribbon
Lace trims
Lace medallions
Embroidered ribbons and trims
Sew-on, machine-embroidered appliqués
Buttons
Tiny pearl and metallic beads
Tiny silk ribbon roses
Lace-edged or embroidered hankies or table linens
Small tatted or crocheted doilies
Brass or silver charms
Small pieces of second-hand jewelry
Eyelet and lace fabrics (layer over a piece of lining fabric)

Embroider web and spider.

Quilt

Presidents' Day

Color photo on page 22

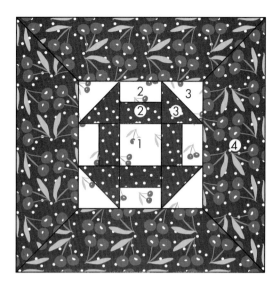

Presidents' Day, the third Monday in February, celebrates the birthdays of Presidents Lincoln and Washington. Use any cherry print for the border to represent President Washington and select fabrics that match for the Lincoln's Platform square. Hang the quilt on the actual birthdays of Lincoln (February 12) and Washington (February 22) in addition to the national holiday.

(The quilt in the color photograph is slightly smaller than 12" square; the border was cut to take advantage of the print.)

Materials 44"-wide fabric

$\frac{1}{8}$ yd. for background
$\frac{1}{8}$ yd. black dot for block
$\frac{1}{4}$ yd. cherry print for border
13" square of batting
$\frac{1}{2}$ yd. for backing
$\frac{1}{4}$ yd. for binding

Cutting

Fabric	Piece No.	No. of Pieces	Dimensions
Background	1	1	$2\frac{1}{2}$" x $2\frac{1}{2}$"
	2	4	$1\frac{1}{2}$" x $2\frac{1}{2}$"
	3	2	$2\frac{7}{8}$" x $2\frac{7}{8}$" ◻
Black dot	2	4	$1\frac{1}{2}$" x $2\frac{1}{2}$"
	3	2	$2\frac{7}{8}$" x $2\frac{7}{8}$" ◻
Cherry print for border	4	4	$3\frac{1}{2}$" x $13\frac{1}{4}$"

Assembly

1. Sew a black dot 2 to a background 2.

Make 4

2. Sew a black dot 3 to a background 3.

Make 4

3. Assemble the units made in steps 1 and 2, and background 1 to make the Lincoln's Platform block.

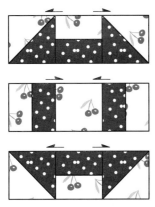

4. Trim both ends of each cherry print border piece at a 45° angle, using a Bias Square or the 45° angle on your rotary ruler. Be sure to trim from the exact corner so that the long side of the piece still measures 13¼" after trimming.

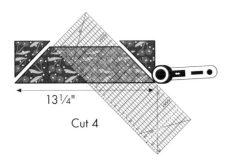

13¼"

Cut 4

5. Sew a border to each side of the block, beginning and ending your stitching within ¼" of the block corners and backstitching. To miter the corners, match the diagonal edges of the borders and sew ¼" seams from the inside corner to the outer edge.

Finishing

Refer to pages 16–19 to finish your quilt.

1. Layer the quilt top with 13" squares of batting and backing. Trim the batting and backing so they extend ¼" beyond the quilt top. Baste.
2. Quilt in-the-ditch around the Lincoln's Platform design and around the edge of the block inside the border.
3. Bind the edges.

On March 17, the Irish celebrate St. Patrick, who brought Christianity to Ireland and is credited with many feats, including driving out all the snakes. These three snakes, commemorating the event, are created with Bargello strip piecing.

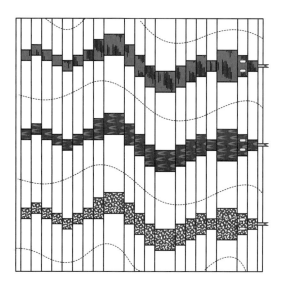

Materials: 44"-wide fabric

⅛ yd. each of 3 greens (X, Y, Z) for snakes
⅓ yd. for background
13" square of batting
½ yd. for backing
¼ yd. for binding
6 brass beads, round or rectangular, 3mm to 6mm
3" pink ribbon, ⅛" wide

Cutting and Piecing Strip Units

Refer to Speed Piecing on page 11.

The quilt is made from 20 segments: 9 segments cut from strip unit A (narrow snake segments), 10 segments cut from strip unit B (wide snake segments), and 1 head strip. Decide on the arrangement of your three snake fabrics (X, Y, and Z) before you make the strip units.

1. For strip unit A, cut the following:
   1 strip of each snake green, 1" x 10"
   2 strips background, each 3¾" x 10"
   2 strips background, each 3½" x 10"
2. Assemble the strip unit as shown, with the 3¾"-wide background strips on the inside and the 3½"-wide background strips on the ends.

Note: Strip unit diagrams show cut dimensions.

3. Cut 9 segments, each 1" wide.

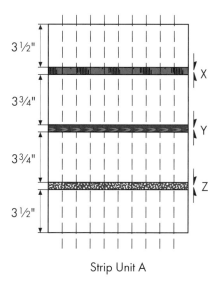

Strip Unit A

4. For strip unit B, cut the following:
   1 strip of each snake green, 1½" x 12"
   2 strips background, each 3¼" x 12"
   2 strips background, each 3½" x 12"
5. Assemble the strip unit as shown, with the 3¼"-wide background strips on the inside and the 3½"-wide background strips on the ends.

6. Cut 8 segments, each 1" wide, and 2 segments, each 1½" wide.

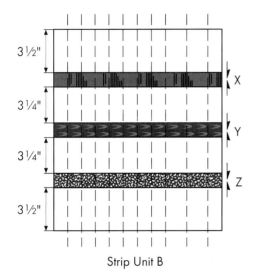

3½"

3¼" — X

3¼" — Y

3½" — Z

Strip Unit B

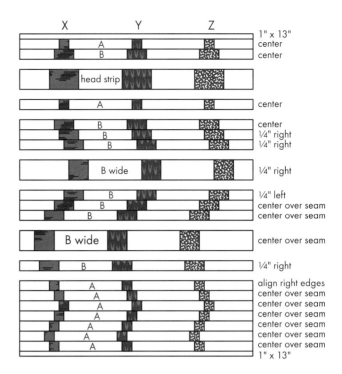

X   Y   Z

1" x 13"
center
center
head strip
center
center
¼" right
¼" right
¼" right
¼" left
center over seam
center over seam
center over seam
¼" right
align right edges
center over seam
center over seam
center over seam
center over seam
center over seam
center over seam
1" x 13"

7. For the head strip, cut the following:
   1 piece of each snake green, 1½" x 2"
   2 pieces background, each 1½" x 2¾"
   2 pieces background, each 1½" x 2"

Note: If you are using any directional prints, be sure the print in the head piece is aligned with the rest of the snake.

8. Assemble the head strip as shown, with the 2¾"-wide background pieces on the inside and the 2"-wide background pieces on the ends.

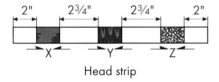

2"   2¾"   2¾"   2"

X   Y   Z

Head strip

9. Cut 2 background strips, each 1" x 13".

Assembly

Note: The segments have extra background fabric on the ends; this will be cut away after the design is assembled and the piece is trimmed to a 12½" square. The background strips that will be added to the nose and tail ends are also cut larger, in case extra fabric is needed when the piece is trimmed before quilting.

1. Following the piecing diagram, arrange the A, B, and head strips in order as shown, with the nose strip on top and the tip of the tail on the bottom.

2. Starting with the head strip, position each strip relative to the strip just above it. Move the strip either left or right, or center it as indicated; pin in place and stitch. Continue adding strips toward the tail, then go back to the head strip and work upward. Press each seam allowance after stitching to help keep the piece flat as you sew. Press all the seam allowances in one direction.

3. Add the 1" x 13" background strips to the ends.

4. Trim the piece to 12½" x 12½". Use the head strip as a guide; it should be exactly 12½" wide. The head of the center snake (nose through neck) is in the exact center of the piece. Notice that the tail of the center snake is not in the center. Snakes actually travel sideways rather than straight ahead (hence the term "sidewinder"), and they look like this when they move.

Finishing

Refer to pages 16–19 to finish your quilt.

1. Layer the quilt top with 13" squares of batting and backing. Trim the batting and backing so they extend ¼" beyond the quilt top. Baste.

2. Quilt in smooth curves, following the shape of the snakes.

3. Bind the edges.

4. Sew on bead eyes.

5. Cut 3 ribbon tongues, ¾" long. Cut a deep V in each tongue. Tack straight ends to snake noses.

Quilt
Swallows' Return

Color photo on page 22

Each year on March 19, cliff swallows return from their winter grounds in South America to nest at San Juan Capistrano, a Franciscan mission in Southern California. This appliqué quilt, which depicts the brown swallows returning to the mission in the center of the block, is based on the traditional Swallow block.

Materials: 44"-wide fabric

1/8 yd. brown print for swallows
1/4 yd. off-white print for center
2/3 yd. for background (includes binding)
13" square of batting
1/2 yd. for backing (optional)*

I made my quilt reversible with the "Buzzards' Return" quilt (opposite page), so I did not need a backing.

Cutting

Fabric	Piece No.	No. of Pieces	Dimensions
Brown print	T1	4	
	T2	4 + 4r	
Off-white print	T3	1	
Background		1	12½" x 12½"

Assembly

Refer to Paper-Patch Appliqué on page 14. Use templates on page 99.

1. Paper-patch templates T1, T2, and T3.

2. Whipstitch a paper-patched T2 to each side of a T1.

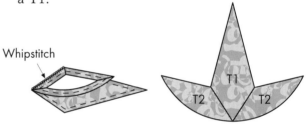

Whipstitch

3. Fold the background square on both diagonals and lightly crease the folds. Center T3 on the background square, placing the 4 points of T3 on the diagonals. Appliqué in place.

4. Position the T1/T2 units at the 4 corners of T3, lining up each unit on a diagonal so that the rounded edge touches the point of T3. Appliqué in place.

Finishing

Refer to pages 16—19 to finish your quilt.

1. Layer the quilt top with 13" squares batting and backing. "Buzzards' Return" may be used for the back to make a reversible quilt (see hint on page 44).Trim the batting and backing so they extend 1/4" beyond the quilt top. Baste.

2. Quilt around T3 and the T1/T2 units. Quilt a mission bell in the center of T3.

3. Bind the edges.

On March 15, buzzards (more correctly, turkey vultures) return from their winter grounds in the southern United States to nest around Hinckley, Ohio. The patient vulture in the quilt is foundation-pieced, while the graceful, soaring vulture is appliquéd and embroidered.

Buzzard Block: 7" x 7½"

Materials: 44"-wide fabric

Scraps of 2 black solid or print fabrics for vultures
Scrap of brown fabric for branch
½ yd. for background (includes binding)
13" square of batting
½ yd. for backing
Gray and black embroidery floss

Cutting

Note: Cut the binding strips and rectangles from the background fabric first. Use the remainder for foundation piecing.

Fabric	Piece No.	No. of Pieces	Dimensions
Black	T1	1	
	T2	1	
Background		1	5½" x 7"
		1	6" x 12½"

Assembly

Refer to Foundation Piecing on page 12 and Paper-Patch Appliqué on page 14. Use templates below and block design on page 100.

1. Foundation-piece the sitting vulture in sections. Assemble the sections in numerical order. Then sew A to B; C to A/B; A/B/C to D, and so forth. Press well. Trim to 7" wide and 7½" tall.
2. Sew the 5½" x 7" background piece to the top of the vulture. Add the 6" x 12½" background piece to the right side. Remove the foundation paper. Embroider the vulture's eye and a line along the front edge of the wing.
3. Paper-patch T1 and T2, turning under 3 edges of tail (T2) and leaving the top edge raw. Appliqué the soaring vulture in place, tucking the raw edge of the tail under the body. Embroider feathers at the wing tips.

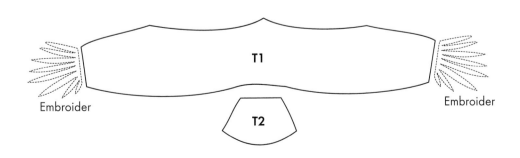

Embroider   T1   Embroider

T2

Finishing

Refer to pages 16–19 to finish your quilt.

1. Layer the quilt top with 13" squares of batting and backing. Swallows' return may be used for the back to make a reversible quilt (see hint at right). Trim the batting and backing so they extend ¼" beyond the quilt top. Baste.
2. Quilt wind curls in the sky.
3. Bind the edges.

Hint

Small Reversible Quilts

"Swallows' Return" and "Buzzards' Return," having similar themes, make an amusing reversible quilt. In a reversible quilt, there are two elements that show on both sides: the binding and the quilting. In this case, you can solve the binding problem by using the same sky background fabric or two compatible blues.

The quilting is a more difficult problem, because both quilts are pictorial. Instead of settling for a quilting design that works on one side and conflicts with the design on the other side, you can use two squares of thin batting and quilt each top separately. Use a stable batting, such as thin Pellon, so you can eliminate the bulk of two backs; simply layer the top and the batting, baste, and quilt. Then place the two quilts wrong sides together and bind.

January • February • **March** • April • May • **June** • July • August • **September** • October • November • **December**

Quilt

Solstice/Equinox Quilt

Color photo on page 23

Celebrate the summer and winter solstices and the spring and fall equinoxes with one quilt. Hang the quilt so the appropriate astrological sign is at the top of the quilt: the ram (Aries) for the vernal equinox, March 20 or 21; the crab (Cancer) for the summer solstice, June 20 or 21; the scales (Libra) for the autumnal equinox, September 22 or 23; or the goat (Capricorn) for the winter solstice, December 21 or 22. The sun in the background is embroidered in metallic gold thread. You could duplicate the dramatic black and gold of the sample quilt, or you could use a sky-blue background and seasonal colors for the astrological signs: greens for spring, bright colors for summer, golds for autumn, and white for winter.

Materials: 44"-wide fabric

¼ yd. main fabric for astrological symbols
Scrap for ram horn fabric
Scrap of UltraSuede for goat horns
⅓ yd. for background (includes binding)
13" square of batting
½ yd. for backing
Metallic gold thread
Tan, brown, and black embroidery floss
2 gold, ⅛"-diameter beads for crab eyes

Assembly

Refer to Paper-Patch Appliqué on page 14. For the placement of each astrological sign, refer to the quilt diagram (opposite) or the color photo on page 23. Use templates on pages 102–103.

1. Fold a 12½" square piece of paper in half, then in half again. Trace the one-quarter sun design on page 102 onto the paper, aligning the placement lines with the crease lines on the paper. Repeat 3 more times, rotating the design as necessary to complete the sun design. Transfer the design to a 12½" square of background fabric. Hand or machine embroider the design in metallic gold thread.

2. **Ram:** Paper-patch T1 and T3 from the main fabric, and T2 from the ram horn fabric. Appliqué the ram head (T1) in place. Embroider the features. Appliqué the horn (T2) in place. Embroider the outer edge and the curl, using 2 strands of embroidery floss. Embroider the cross ridges, using 1 strand of embroidery floss. Appliqué the ram ear (T3) in place.

3. **Crab:** Paper-patch T4–T12 and T5r–T11r from the main fabric. Baste body (T4) in place, then position legs (T5, T6, T7, T5r, T6r, T7r) under the body and appliqué in place. Appliqué the body. Pin leg segments (T8–T12, T8r–T11r) in place and then appliqué, starting with claw pincers (T11, T11r) and ending with segment T8, T8r tucking each piece under the next piece to be appliquéd. Embroider the eye stalks and sew the gold beads to the ends.

4. **Scales:** Paper-patch T13, T14, and two T15 from the main fabric. Appliqué stand (T13) in place, then crossbar (T14) and pans (T15). Embroider the cords from the crossbar to the pans.

5. **Goat:** Paper-patch head (T16) and 2 ears (T17) from the main fabric. Cut 2 horns (T18) from UltraSuede. Pin head (T16) in place. Slip 1 ear and 1 horn under the head and appliqué in place. Appliqué the head and the remaining horn and ear. Embroider the features and the beard.

Finishing

Refer to pages 16–19 to finish your quilt.

1. Layer the quilt top with 13" squares of batting and backing. Trim the batting and backing so they extend ¼" beyond the quilt top. Baste.
2. Quilt around each astrological sign.
3. Bind the edges.

Quilt

April Showers

Color photo on page 23

Choose your favorite floral print for the background and use shades of one of the colors for your umbrella. Quilt glistening lines of rain with metallic silver thread.

Materials: 44"-wide fabric

⅛ yd. each of 2 umbrella fabrics (A and B)
½ yd. floral for background
13" square of batting
½ yd. for backing
¼ yd. for binding
Metallic silver thread

Cutting

Fabric	Piece No.	No. of Pieces	Dimensions
Fabric A	T1	4	
	T2	1	
	T3	1	
Fabric B	T1	3	
Background		1	12½" x 12½"

Assembly

Refer to Paper-Patch Appliqué on page 14. Use templates on page 102.

1. Paper-patch umbrella pieces T1, T2, and T3.

2. Sew T1 pieces together side by side, alternating the colors. Place the pieces right sides together and whipstitch them together in pairs, then whipstitch the pairs together. Add the seventh segment.

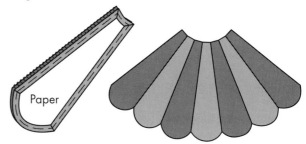

3. Whipstitch T2 to the top of the umbrella.
4. Pin the umbrella in place on the background square. Center the umbrella handle below the umbrella, tucking the raw edge under the bottom edge of the umbrella. Appliqué the handle, then the umbrella, removing the paper as you go.

Finishing

Refer to pages 16–19 to finish your quilt.

1. Layer the quilt top with 13" squares of batting and backing. Trim the batting and backing so they extend ¼" beyond the quilt top. Baste.
2. Quilt around the umbrella and handle. Using metallic silver thread, quilt rain lines above the umbrella.
3. Bind the edges.

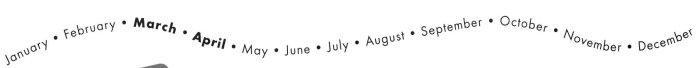

Quilt

The Easter Tree

Color photo on page 23

When I was a child, every year for weeks, we blew eggs and rinsed and dried them, saving them to decorate and hang on our egg tree for Easter. These eggs are strip- and foundation-pieced in pretty spring pastels; you could also make an Easter egg tree in deeper jewel tones and gilded fabrics.

Materials: 44"-wide fabric

Assorted scraps of solids and prints for eggs
⅛ yd. fabric for tree
½ yd. for background
13" square of batting
½ yd. for backing
¼ yd. for binding
Pink embroidery floss

Assembly

Refer to Speed Piecing on page 11, and String Piecing, Spiral Crazy Patchwork, and Paper-Patch Appliqué on page 14. Use templates on page 101.

Note: Strip-unit diagrams show cut dimensions of each strip.

Tree

1. Paper-patch tree pieces T2–T6 and T2r–T4r. Turn under all edges of the branches except the short straight edges, which will be covered by the trunk (T6).
2. Cut a 12½" x 12½" square from the background fabric. Arrange the branches and trunk on the square, referring to the quilt diagram above right.
3. Appliqué the tree branches in numerical order, slipping the raw edge of the branches under the tree trunk.

Egg A (make 2 different color combinations)

1. From assorted fabrics, cut 3 strips, each ¾" x 6". From a fourth fabric, cut 2 strips, each 1" x 6", and 2 pieces, each 1¼" x 2½".
2. Sew the 6" strips together in the order shown. Cut 7 segments, each ¾" wide.

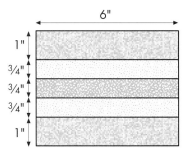

3. Sew the segments together in pairs, staggering the pieces as shown and matching seams. Sew the pairs and seventh segment together to make one pieced strip.

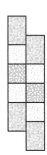

4. Align the ¼" line on a rotary ruler with the points of the upper and lower rows of squares. Trim along the edge of the ruler, leaving a ¼"-wide seam allowance.

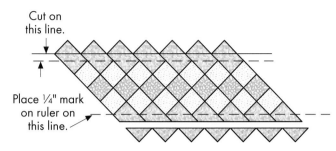

Cut on this line.

Place ¼" mark on ruler on this line.

5. Sew the 1¼" x 2½" pieces to the top and bottom of the pieced strip.

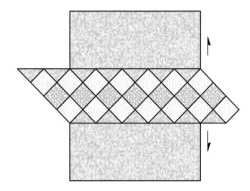

6. Prepare paper-patch appliqué with egg (T1).

Egg B (make 2 different color combinations)
1. From each of 2 different fabrics, cut 2 strips, each 1" x 10". Sew the strips together, alternating fabrics as shown. Cut 7 segments at a 45° angle, each ¾" wide.

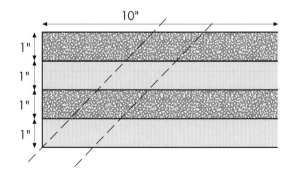

10"

1"

1"

1"

1"

2. Sew the segments together in pairs, matching long edges and lining up the tips of the segments as shown.

Line up points.

3. Sew the pairs and the seventh segment together to make one pieced strip.

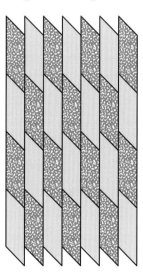

4. Prepare paper-patch appliqué with egg (T1).

Egg C (make 2 different color combinations)

Trace T1 onto foundation paper. Starting at one end of the egg, string-piece irregular strips of fabric to cover T1, leaving a ¼"-wide seam allowance all around. Paper-patch with egg (T1).

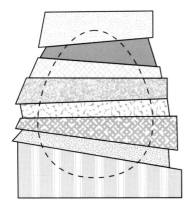

Egg D (make 2 different color combinations)

Trace T1 onto foundation paper. Starting in the center, spiral crazy-piece irregular pieces of fabric to cover T1, leaving a ¼"-wide seam allowance all around. Paper-patch with egg (T1).

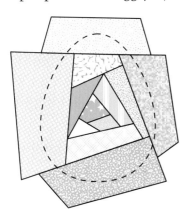

Egg E (make 1)

Trace T1 onto foundation paper, copying the lengthwise placement line. Foundation-piece strips of fabric from one side of the egg to the other, leaving a ¼"-wide seam allowance all around. Use the lengthwise line to keep all the seam lines parallel. Paper-patch with egg (T1).

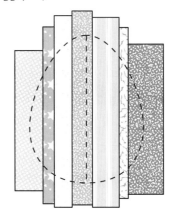

Egg F (make 1)

Follow the directions for Egg E, but use the crosswise placement line on T1.

Egg G (make 3)

Paper-patch the remaining 3 eggs, using a different print fabric for each egg (or make 3 more eggs from designs A–F).

Appliqué the eggs, placing each hanging egg slightly below the branch. Embroider the thread loops.

Finishing

Refer to pages 16–19 to finish your quilt.
1. Layer the quilt top with 13" squares of batting and backing. Trim the batting and backing so they extend ¼" beyond the quilt top. Baste.
2. Quilt around the tree branches and trunk.
3. Bind the edges.

Quilt

Trees 'n' Breeze

Color photo on page 24

Arbor Day, a day to celebrate the beauty of trees and to plant a few, is generally celebrated on the last Friday in April. This quilt can also celebrate Earth Day, first held on April 22, 1970, and recognized annually in many regions of the country with a variety of environmental activities. United Nations World Environment Day is celebrated June 5. Tu B'Sh'vat, the fifteenth day of the month of Shebat on the Jewish calendar (late January or early February) is the New Year of the Trees, a day to celebrate trees and the natural world. The quilt can also be fancied up for Christmas (see the Hint box on page 51).

This is a speedy design based on the Log Cabin block. Once you have string-pieced the fabric for the trees, it goes together very quickly. Or, for a really quick quilt, omit the string piecing altogether; striped fabrics will produce a similar effect.

Materials: 44"-wide fabric

Scraps of 10 or more green fabrics for leaves
Scraps of 5 brown fabrics for trunks
¼ yd. for background
13" square of batting
½ yd. for backing
¼ yd. for binding

Cutting

Fabric	Piece No.	No. of Pieces	Dimensions
Asst. browns	3	5	1" x 2½"
Background	strip units	5	2½" x 10"
	1	3	2½" x 2½" ◻
	2	5	3" x 3" ◻
	4	2	2½" x 6½"

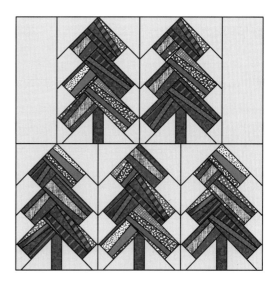

Tree Block: 4" x 6"

Assembly

Refer to String Piecing on page 14.

1. For each tree, cut a 3¼" x 10" foundation from paper or muslin. Cover with irregular, narrow strips of green fabrics. Use a different combination of green fabrics for each tree. Trim to 3¼" x 10".

2. Sew a 2½" x 10" background piece to the foundation-pieced green strip unit. Crosscut the unit into 6 segments, each 1½" wide.

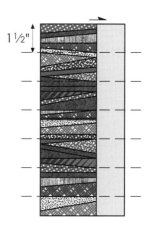

1½"

3. For each branch (A–F), trim the amount listed below from the green end of the segment.

Segment	Amount to Cut
A	1"
B	0
C	1¼"
D	¼"
E	1¾"
F	¾"

4. Sew a background 1 to each long edge of brown 3. Trim the top of the trunk to a point. Prepare 5 trunk units, one for each tree.

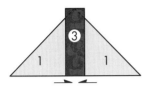

5. Following the diagrams, sew tree strip A to a trunk unit and press. Add tree strips B–F in order, pressing after adding each strip. Add a background 2 to each side of the tree top.

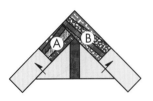

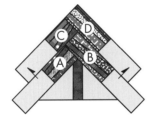

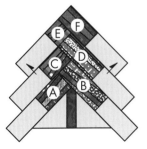

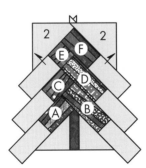

6. Trim the block to 4½" x 6½", centering the trunk within the 4½" and leaving a ¼"-wide seam allowance at the top of the tree. Make 5 trees.

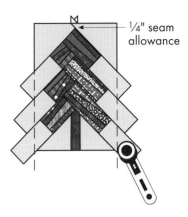

¼" seam allowance

7. Sew 3 trees together for the bottom row. Sew 2 trees together and add a background 4 to each side for the top row. Join the rows to complete the quilt top.

Finishing

Refer to pages 16–19 to finish your quilt.

1. Layer the quilt top with 13" squares of batting and backing. Trim the batting and backing so they extend ¼" beyond the quilt top. Baste.
2. Quilt in-the-ditch around each tree.
3. Bind the edges.

Hint

For a Christmas quilt, decorate each tree with brass charms, tiny ornaments from the miniature section of a craft store, tiny bows, sequins, and beads. For a country look, decorate each tree with tiny buttons. Or make a quilt of "family trees" for Christmas, decorating each tree with charms and ornaments that reflect the interests of a particular family member (see "Family Trees" on page 95).

Quilt

Cinco de Mayo

Color photo on page 24

Cinco de Mayo (Fifth of May) celebrates the decisive victory of the Mexican army over the French at Pueblo, Mexico, on May 5, 1862. Other holidays to celebrate include Mexican Independence Day (September 16) and National Hispanic Heritage Month (September 15–October 15).

This little quilt, in bright Southwest colors, is made of four traditional Mexican Star blocks assembled in a speedy, nontraditional way.

Mexican Star Block: 6"

Materials: 44"-wide fabric

¼ yd. orange
¼ yd. yellow
¼ yd. gold (includes binding)
⅛ yd. turquoise
13" square of batting
½ yd. for backing

Cutting

Note: Some of the pieces you cut may not look like the corresponding pieces in the block diagram because some of the diagonals are speed-pieced and because the star will be sewn together and then cut into pieces. The diagram shows you the location of each piece, not necessarily its actual shape.

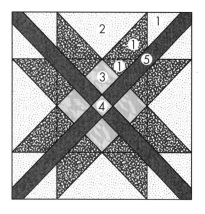

Fabric	Piece No.	No. of Pieces	Dimensions
Orange	1	48	2" x 2"
Yellow	1	16	2" x 2"
	2	16	2" x 3½"
Gold	3	4	3½" x 3½"
	4	4	1" x 1"
Turquoise	5	16	1" x 5"

Assembly

1. Speed-piece an orange 1 to opposite ends of a yellow 2. Make 4 units for each star (16 total).

 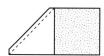 

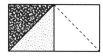 

2. Speed-piece an orange 1 to each corner of a gold 3. Sew opposite corners, trim, and press, then sew remaining corners. Make 4 units, one for each star.

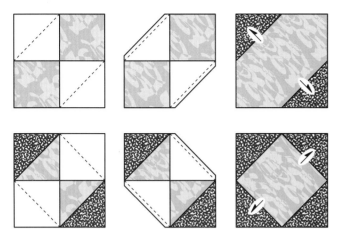

3. Assemble 4 star blocks as shown.

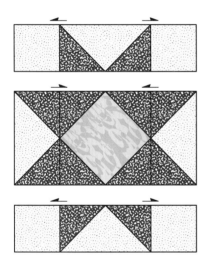

4. Cut each star block twice diagonally, making 4 triangle units from each star.

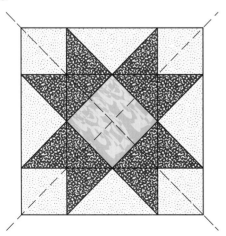

5. Sew a turquoise 5 between each pair of triangle units.

6. Sew a turquoise 5 to opposite sides of gold 4. Make 4 units. Sew these between 2 triangle units to complete 1 star. Make 4 stars.

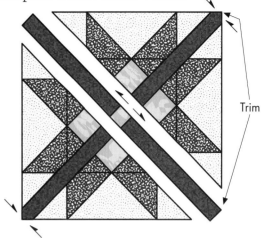

7. Sew the 4 stars together.

Finishing

Refer to pages 16–19 to finish your quilt.
1. Layer the quilt top with 13" squares of batting and backing. Trim the batting and backing so they extend ¼" beyond the quilt top. Baste.
2. Quilt in diagonal lines down the center of the turquoise strips.
3. Bind the edges.

Hint
Matching Triangle Points
It can be difficult to accurately match triangle points when there is a lot of bulk from seam allowances. To match two triangle points, place one directly above the other, right sides together, and push a pin vertically through the exact tips of the two triangles. With that pin in place, pin the two pieces together on either side of the center pin. Remove the center pin and sew.

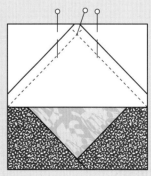

Quilt

Kentucky Derby Day

Color photo on page 24

The Kentucky Derby, the first race of the annual Triple Crown, is always the first Saturday in May.

The horse has many odd-shaped pieces—43 all together—but because it is foundation-pieced, there are no templates. Ten different sections are foundation-pieced and then sewn together. If you are new to foundation piecing, you might want to try a simpler block, such as the cat (page 59) or the leaf (page 76), before tackling this design.

Horse Block: 8"

Materials: 44"-wide fabrics

⅛ yd. fabric for horse
Scrap of matching fabric for mane and tail
¼ yd. for background (includes inner border)
⅛ yd. for outer border
13" square of batting
½ yd. for backing
¼ yd. for binding

Cutting

Note: Cut the inner border strips from the background fabric first, then use the remainder for foundation piecing.

Fabric		No. of Pieces	Dimensions
Background	top/bottom	2	1¼" x 8½"
	sides	2	1¼" x 10"
Outer border	top/bottom	2	1¾" x 10"
	sides	2	1¾" x 12½"

Assembly

Refer to Foundation Piecing on page 12. Use 8" Horse block design on pages 104–105.

1. Foundation-piece the sections of the horse, adding fabrics in numerical order.
2. Join the sections as follows:
    Sew A to B.
    Sew C to A/B.
    Sew D to E.
    Sew D/E to A/B/C.
    Sew F to G.
    Sew I to H.
    Sew F/G to H/I.
    Sew J to F/G/H/I.
    Sew the horse back to the horse front.
3. Trim the horse to 8½" x 8½".
4. Add the inner border strips to the top and bottom, then to the sides.
5. Add the outer border strips to the top and bottom, then to the sides.

Finishing

Refer to pages 16–19 to finish your quilt.

1. Layer the quilt top with 13" squares of batting and backing. Trim the batting and backing so they extend ¼" beyond the quilt top. Baste.
2. Quilt in-the-ditch between the inner and outer borders.
3. Bind the edges.

Quilt

Be Kind to Animals

Color photo on page 25

Celebrate our furry and scaly friends during Be-Kind-to-Animals Week, the first week of May, with foundation-pieced rabbits, cats, frogs, fish, a dog, and an appliquéd, side-winding snake.

Rabbit Block: 2³/₄" x 4"   **Cat Block: 3" x 5¹/₄"**
Frog Block: 3³/₄" x 2"   **Dog Block: 4¹/₂" x 6"**
                          Fish Block: ³/₄" x 3"

Materials: 44"-wide fabric

¹/₃ yd. for background
¹/₄ yd. underwater blue (includes binding)
Assorted scraps of grays and browns for rabbits, cats, and dog
Assorted scraps of greens for frogs, snake, fish, and lily pad strip
13" square of batting
¹/₂ yd. for backing
Seed beads, 3mm beads, and 5mm split beads for eyes and dog nose

Cutting

Note: Cut the background pieces first, then use the remainder for foundation piecing.

Fabric	Piece No.	No. of Pieces	Dimensions
Background	1	1	2¹/₂" x 6"
	2	1	1" x 5³/₄"
	3	1	1¹/₄" x 7"
Underwater blue	4	2	1¹/₄" x 8"
	5	2	1¹/₄" x 2³/₄"
	6	1	1¹/₄" x 2"
Green	4	1	1¹/₄" x 8"
	T1	1	

Assembly

Refer to Foundation Piecing on page 12 and Paper-Patch Appliqué on page 14. Use template and block designs on pages 106–107. The fish block design is on page 62.

1. Foundation-piece 2 rabbits; 2 cats, 1 and 1 reversed; 1 dog; 2 frogs; and 3 fish. For the fish only, use the underwater blue as the background fabric.

2. Assemble the lily pad strip and underwater pieces as shown.

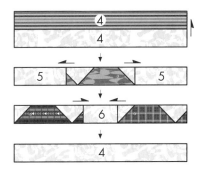

3. Paper-patch the snake (T1). Appliqué to background 1.

4. Assemble the quilt in sections as shown.

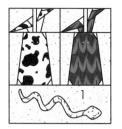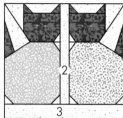
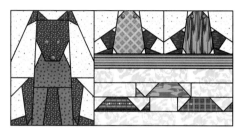

Finishing

Refer to pages 16–19 to finish your quilt.

1. Layer the quilt top with 13" squares of batting and backing. Trim the batting and backing so they extend ¼" beyond the quilt top. Baste.
2. Quilt around all the animals. Quilt a few wavy lines in the underwater scene.
3. Bind the edges.
4. Sew on seed beads for snake, fish, rabbit, and cat eyes. Sew on 3mm beads for dog eyes. Glue on 5mm split beads for frog eyes and dog nose.

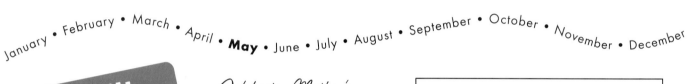

January • February • March • April • **May** • June • July • August • September • October • November • December

Quilt

Mother's Day

Color photo on page 25

Celebrate Mother's Day, the second Sunday in May, with a quilt of traditional Duck and Ducklings blocks. Personalize your quilt with novelty prints representing the ducklings in your family. Don't forget Mother-in-Law Day as well, October 22.

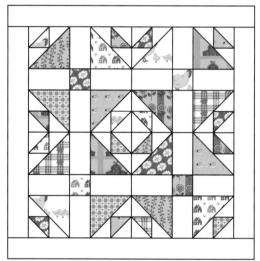

Duck and Duckings Block: 6"

Materials: 44"-wide fabric

Assorted scraps of novelty prints for blocks
¼ yd. for background and border (or scraps of several backgrounds)
13" square of batting
½ yd. for backing
¼ yd. for binding

Cutting

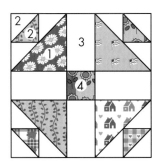

Fabric	Piece No.	No. of Pieces	Dimensions
Asst. novelty prints	1	8	2⅞" x 2⅞" ◰
	2	8	1⅞" x 1⅞" ◰
	4	4	1½" x 1½"
Background	2	24	1⅞" x 1⅞" ◰
	3	16	1½" x 2½"
Borders	sides	2	1½" x 10½"
	top/bottom	2	1½" x 12½"

Assembly

1. Sew novelty print 2 to a background 2. Then add a background 2 to each side of the novelty print 2. Sew each unit to a novelty print 1.

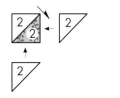

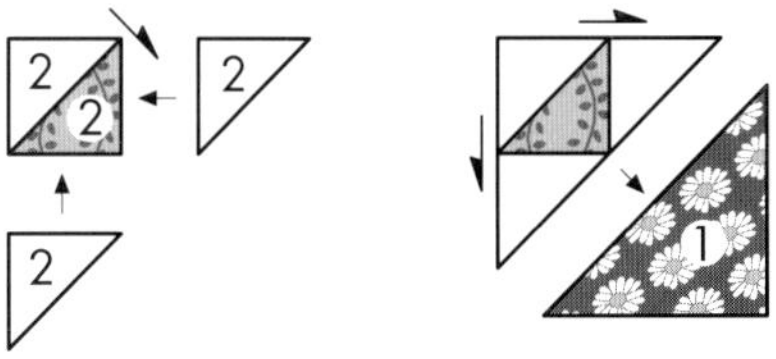

2. Sew a background 3 to opposite sides of a novelty print 4.

3. Assemble 4 Duck and Ducklings blocks, following the piecing diagram.

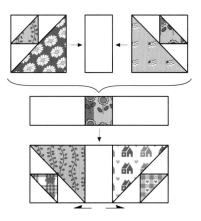

4. Sew the 4 blocks together.
5. Add the border strips to the sides, then to the top and bottom.

Finishing

Refer to pages 16–19 to finish your quilt.

1. Layer the quilt top with 13" squares of batting and backing. Trim the batting and backing so they extend ¼" beyond the quilt top. Baste.
2. Quilt in-the-ditch along the seams joining the 4 blocks and inside the border strips.
3. Bind the edges.

Hint
Cutting Novelty Prints

It can be difficult to precisely place a novelty-print design when the triangles and squares are as small as they are in this quilt. To help center the designs, cut clear-plastic templates for pieces 1, 2, and 4. After you have placed each template, either cut around the template carefully with your rotary cutter, or draw around the template and cut the piece out with scissors.

Quilt

Eliza Doolittle Day

Color photo on page 25

"Next week, on the twentieth of May, I proclaim 'Liza Doolittle Day!'" So sang the king in Eliza's daydream in "My Fair Lady." Remember Eliza Doolittle, the cockney flower girl, with a bouquet of delicate appliquéd violets. Although the violets can be fused, they look especially nice in traditional appliqué; the pieces are so small that the seam allowances tucked under the petals round them out, softening the design.

Materials: 44"-wide fabric

Assorted scraps of 5 to 10 purple prints and solids
1/4 yd. green for leaves (includes binding)
1/2 yd. for background
13" square of batting
1/2 yd. for backing
Yellow and green embroidery floss
2/3 yd. of 3/8"-wide ribbon for bow

Assembly

Refer to Paper-Patch Appliqué on page 14. Use templates on page 109.

1. For each violet, paper-patch all 5 petals from one fabric. Paper-patch buds from 2 fabrics.
2. Cut a 12½" x 12½" square from background fabric. Fold the fabric in half horizontally and vertically to find the center of the square. Using the diagram on page 109, place the center of the background square on the dot in the center of the diagram. Mark the positions of the violets, buds, and leaves on the background square.
3. Appliqué the paper-patched pieces in place.
4. Stitch a yellow French knot in the center of each violet (see "Embroidery" on page 18).
5. Fold the ribbon in half to find the center. Baste the center 1" of ribbon in place, right side down. Embroider the stems, stitching over the ribbon.

Finishing

Refer to pages 16–19 to finish your quilt.

1. Layer the quilt top with 13" squares of batting and backing. Trim the batting and backing so they extend 1/4" beyond the quilt top. Baste.
2. Quilt a few graceful lines around the bouquet.
3. Bind the edges.
4. Tie the ribbon bow and tack in place.

Quilt
Adopt-a-Shelter-Cat Month

Color photo on page 25

June is Adopt-a-Shelter-Cat Month, and these six foundation pieced cats are looking for a home. Use fabrics that remind you of cats you know, or sew up some fantasy cats.

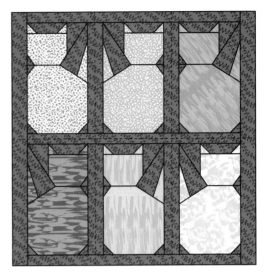

Cat Block: 3" x 5¼"

Materials: 44"-wide fabric

Assorted scraps for 6 cats
¼ yd. for background
13" square of batting
½ yd. for backing
¼ yd. for binding

Cutting

Fabric	Piece No.	No. of Pieces	Dimensions
Background	vertical sashing	4	1¼" x 5¾"
	horizontal sashing	3	1" x 11"
	side borders	2	1¼" x 12½"

Assembly

Refer to Foundation Piecing on page 12. Use block design on page 106.

1. Foundation-piece the head and body units for 6 cats. Make 3 cats as illustrated and 3 reversed.
2. Sew the head unit to the body unit in 2 steps. With right sides facing, pin together at A and B. Sew from A to B, backstitching at B. Remove the piece from the machine. Snip the paper foundation on the head unit to the seam line at point B. Pin the seam at B and C. Sew from C to B, backstitching at B. Trim each cat to 3½" x 5¾".
3. Arrange the cats in 2 rows of 3 blocks each. Sew vertical sashing strips between cats in each row.
4. Sew the horizontal sashing strips between the rows, and to the top and bottom of the quilt.
5. Add the side border strips.
6. Remove the paper foundations.

Finishing

Refer to pages 16–19 to finish your quilt.

1. Layer the quilt top with 13" squares of batting and backing. Trim the batting and backing so they extend ¼" beyond the quilt top. Baste.
2. Quilt down the centers of the vertical sashing strips and the center horizontal strip.
3. Bind the edges.

Hint
Embellishing Your Cats

Tack a fabric or ribbon bow to each cat, or a ribbon with a bell threaded on it. Or better yet, give them collars with tags so they'll never be lost again. If you want to add whiskers and eyes, place them both just below the midline of the cat's face and make the eyes small.

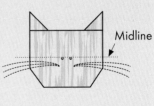

Midline

Quilt

Flag Day

Color photo on page 26

This is a very simple quilt to piece. Use a narrow red-and-white striped fabric for the flags and two navy blue fabrics: one with small stars for the flags, and a matching fabric with larger stars for the border.

The quilt can be hung on any patriotic holiday and to commemorate a number of lesser-known events: patriots' birthdays (Thomas Paine, January 29; Nathan Hale, June 6), the date the national anthem was adopted (March 3), John Philip Sousa's birthday (November 6), and election day (the first Tuesday after the first Monday in November).

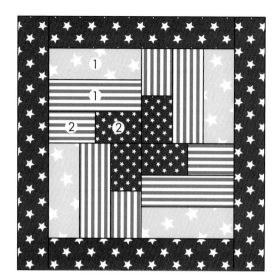

Materials : 44"-wide fabric

½ yd. red-and-white stripe for flags (includes binding)
⅛ yd. navy blue with small stars for flags
⅛ yd. for background
¼ yd. navy blue with larger stars for border
13" square of batting
½ yd. for backing

Cutting

Fabric	Piece No.	No. of Pieces	Dimensions
Red-and-white stripe	1	4	2" x 5"
	2	4	2" x 2¾"
Navy blue, small stars	2	4	2" x 2¾"
Background	1	4	2" x 5"
Navy blue, borders	top/bottom	2	2" x 9½"
	sides	2	2" x 12½"

Assembly

1. Sew a red stripe 2 to a navy blue 2 on the short sides. Add a red stripe 1 and a background 1 to complete the flag unit. Make 4 flag units.

2. Sew 4 flag units together, rotating them as shown.

3. Add the top and bottom borders, then the side borders.

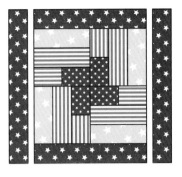

Finishing

Refer to pages 16–19 to finish your quilt.
1. Layer the quilt top with 13" squares of batting and backing. Trim the batting and backing so they extend ¼" beyond the quilt top. Baste.
2. Machine quilt around each flag and inside the border.
3. Bind with bias strips of the red-and-white striped fabric.

January • February • March • April • May • **June** • July • August • September • October • November • December

Color photo on page 26

This Father's Day quilt depicts a personal memory of my father. Every summer, my family rented a cabin on a large lake in Michigan and went fishing almost every day. When my sisters and I were little, my father would take us to a shallow, weedy area of the lake, where lots of little perch lived, and he would spend the afternoon untangling our lines and taking fish off our hooks and throwing them back because they were too small to keep. I'm sure this wasn't his idea of fishing, but because he was a daddy, he took us where we would have fun and catch lots of fish.

Father's Day is the third Sunday in June. This quilt can also commemorate National Hunting and Fishing Day, September 23. Or make it to remember your own summer vacations.

Materials: 44"-wide fabric

Assorted scraps of green prints for fish
⅓ yd. for water (includes binding)
¼ yd. for sky
13" square of batting
½ yd. for backing

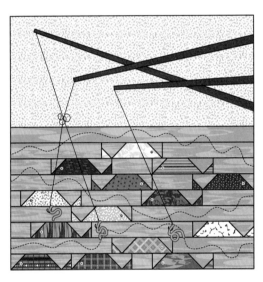

Fish Block: ³/₄" x 3"

Scraps of brown UltraSuede for poles
Lightweight fusible web
Fine nylon thread
Seed beads for fish eyes
Heavyweight black thread
5" "spaghetti" plastic strip or red rubber band for worms*
3 fishhooks, size 10

*Plastic spaghetti is available at craft stores in the leather-kit section.

Cutting

Fabric	Piece No.	No. of Pieces	Dimensions
Water	1	1	1¼" x 1"
	2	2	1¼" x 1½"
	3	5	1¼" x 2½"
	4	1	1¼" x 3"
	5	2	1¼" x 3½"
	6	2	1¼" x 4½"
	7	2	1¼" x 5"
	8	2	1¼" x 5½"
	9	1	1¼" x 6½"
	10	1	1¼" x 12½"
Sky		1	5¾" x 12½"

Assembly

Refer to Foundation Piecing on page 12 and Fusible Appliqué on page 15. Use block design below.

1. Foundation-piece 14 fish, 9 that face left and 5 that face right. Trim each fish to 1¼" x 3½".
2. Sew the fish to the water strips, following the piecing diagram.

3. Sew the fish strips together. Press the seam allowances toward the bottom of the quilt. Remove the foundation papers.
4. Sew the sky piece to the top of the fish section. Press the seam allowance toward the fish section.
5. Cut a 1" x 12" piece of brown UltraSuede. Following package directions, bond fusible web to one side. Cut 3 fishing poles, each about ¼" wide at the base and ⅛" wide at the tip, from the fused UltraSuede.
6. Peel the paper from the back of the UltraSuede poles and arrange the poles on the quilt top. Trim any excess from the wide end of the pole. Remove 2 poles and fuse the remaining pole in place, then fuse the other poles one by one.
7. If necessary, hand or machine appliqué the edges of the fishing poles.

Finishing

Refer to pages 16–19 to finish your quilt.

1. Layer the quilt top with 13" squares of batting and backing. Trim the batting and backing so they extend ¼" beyond the quilt top. Baste.
2. Quilt a few wavy lines in the water.
3. Bind the edges.
4. With nylon thread, sew a bead in place for each fish eye.
5. Cut 3 pieces of heavyweight black thread, each 12" long. For each fishing line, knot the thread and bury the knot in the quilt under the tip of the fishing pole. Knot and tangle together 2 of the lines. Trim each line to the desired length and tie to a fish hook. To hold the fishing lines in place, couch the tangle and each hook with small stitches of fine nylon thread.
6. Cut worms about 1½" long from the plastic spaghetti or from red rubber bands. Put a worm on each hook. Arrange each worm in a wiggle or a loop and couch in place with nylon thread.

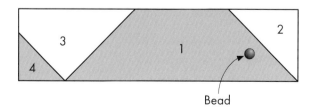

Bead

Quilt

Independence Day

Color photo on page 26

On Independence Day, the Fourth of July, we celebrate the 1776 signing of the Declaration of Independence with spectacular fireworks displays. The fireworks here are shiny beads and sequins, but you can quilt the fireworks in metallic thread or paint them with metallic fabric paints if you prefer.

Materials: 44"-wide fabric

½ yd. muslin for foundation
⅓ yd. red print for striped background (includes binding)
⅛ yd. white print for striped background
⅛ yd. navy blue print for striped background
13" square of batting
½ yd. for backing
Bugle and rocaille beads for fireworks
Large and/or fancy sequins for fireworks

Cutting

Fabric	Piece No.	No. of Pieces	Dimensions
Muslin		1	12½" x 12½"
Red print	1	1	2" x 3"
	5	1	2" x 12"
	9	1	2" x 18"
	13	1	2" x 9"
White print	2	1	1¼" x 4½"
	4	1	1¼" x 9"
	6	1	1¼" x 13½"
	8	1	1¼" x 18"
	10	1	1¼" x 15"
	12	1	1¼" x 10½"
	14	1	1¼" x 6"
	16	1	1¼" x 1½"
Navy blue print	3	1	2" x 8"
	7	1	2" x 16½"
	11	1	2" x 13½"
	15	1	2" x 4½"

Assembly

1. Fold the muslin square in half diagonally and lightly press the fold. Open up and fold the square in half on the other diagonal; lightly press the second fold.

2. Fold red strip 9 in half crosswise and finger-press the fold. Place on the muslin foundation, right side up, centering the fold on the strip with the muslin's diagonal fold line, and the left seam line on the opposite diagonal fold line. Pin in place.

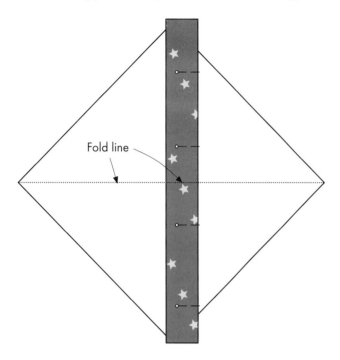

Fold line

3. Fold white strip 10 in half crosswise and finger-press the fold. Place on red strip 9, right sides together and raw edges matching. Place the strip's center fold on the muslin's diagonal line. Sew the seam, using a ¼"-wide seam allowance. Flip the strip open and press.

4. Continue in the same manner, adding strips 11–16 to the right-hand side of the muslin, then start back at the center and add strips 8–1 to the left side. Remember to fold each strip in half and center the fold line on the muslin's diagonal line.

5. Trim the piece to 12½" x 12½".

Finishing

Refer to pages 16–19 to finish your quilt.

1. Layer the quilt top with 13" squares of batting and backing. Trim the batting and backing so they extend ¼" beyond the quilt top. Baste.

2. Quilt a diagonal line in-the-ditch every 2" to 3".

3. Bind the edges.

4. Draw the fireworks designs on pages 110–111 on the quilt with a chalk marker. Quilt the fireworks with metallic thread or use beads and sequins to make the designs (see "Beading" on page 19).

Quilt

Bastille Day

Color photo on page 27

Bastille Day celebrates the beginning of the French Revolution, with the storming of the French prison, the Bastille, by the populace on July 14, 1789. In this Bargello design, representing the reach for freedom, the colors of the French flag seem to gather themselves and soar.

Materials: 44"-wide fabric

1/8 yd. red print for strip units
1/8 yd. white print for strip units
1/3 yd. navy blue print for strip units
   (includes binding)
13" square of batting
1/2 yd. for backing
Metallic silver thread for machine embroidery
Black thread for machine embroidery

Assembly

Refer to Speed Piecing on page 11.

1. From the red, white, and navy blue prints, cut 2 strips, each 1½" x 44". Cut the strips in half at the fold so that you have 4 strips of each fabric, each 1½" wide and at least 22" long.
2. Sew the strips together into a strip unit as shown. Press the seam allowances in one direction.

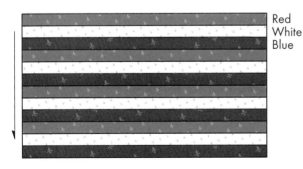

Red
White
Blue

3. Sew the strip unit into a tube and press the seam allowances. Cut the loops in the following sizes and lay them out, still in a loop, in the order cut.

No. to Cut	Size
2	2¼" wide
1	2" wide
1	1¾" wide
1	1½" wide
1	1¼" wide
1	1" wide
10	¾" wide
2	1" wide

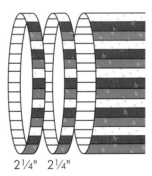

2¼"   2¼"

Note: The loops will be sewn together with the seams staggered so that the seams of each loop fall between the seams of the adjacent loop. To do this, every other loop is opened by removing a seam, and the alternate loops are opened by cutting through the center of a fabric rectangle.

Cut.

4. Start with the first 2¼" loop. Open a seam between a red and a navy blue rectangle, so that a red rectangle is at the top of the loop.
5. Open the second 2¼" loop by cutting through the center of a navy blue rectangle.
6. Proceed down the row of loops, matching the loops to the diagram.

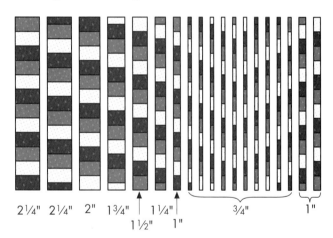

2¼" 2¼" 2" 1¾" 1¼" ¾" 1"
1½" 1"

7. Sew the loops together in the order you cut them, staggering the seams of every other loop. The ends should be even.

Finishing

Refer to pages 16–19 to finish your quilt.

1. Layer the quilt top with 13" squares of batting and backing. Trim the batting and backing so they extend ¼" beyond the quilt top. Baste.
2. With chalk, draw the flag and flagpole. The flag is (from left to right) a navy blue, white, and red rectangle in the second loop. The flagpole extends from the second loop, next to the flag, through the sixth loop.

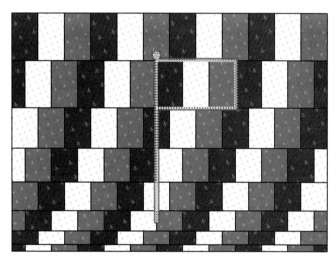

3. With metallic silver thread in the machine, machine embroider the flagpole and around the flag. Sew back and forth 3 or 4 times to make a heavy silver line.
4. With black thread in the machine, machine embroider around the silver embroidery, sewing back and forth 3 or 4 times to make a heavy black line.
5. Bind the edges.

Quilt

Moon Walk

Color photo on page 27

On July 20, 1969, two U.S. astronauts landed Apollo 11's lunar module on the moon and then took a stroll—the first men to walk on the moon. The week around July 20 is designated Space Week and is a time to recognize the accomplishments of space exploration. This little quilt commemorates man's first walk on the moon with a smiling new moon and footprints in lunar dust.

Materials: 44"-wide fabric

¼ yd. navy blue star print for background
⅓ yd. gold print for moon and borders (includes binding)
13" square of batting
½ yd. for backing
¼ yd. fusible web
Black stencil paint for letters and footprints
Black fabric paint for moon eye

Cutting

Fabric	Piece No.	No. of Pieces	Dimensions
Navy blue star print	1	1	8½" x 8½"
Gold print	T1	1	
	T2	1	
	side borders	2	2½" x 8½"
	top/bottom borders	2	2½" x 12½"

Assembly

Refer to Fusible Appliqué on page 15 and Stenciling on page 18. Use templates on page 120.

1. Fuse moon (T1) to navy blue square 1 so that the face is "looking" at the upper right corner of the square.
2. Cut cheek circle (T2) from a contrasting area of the gold print or from a scrap of contrasting fabric. Fuse in place.
3. Add side borders, then top and bottom borders.
4. Stencil "apollo 11" on the left border, and "july 20, 1969" on the bottom border. Stencil footprints on the right and top borders.

Finishing

Refer to pages 16–19 to finish your quilt.

1. Layer the quilt top with 13" squares of batting and backing. Trim the batting and backing so they extend ¼" beyond the quilt top. Baste.
2. Quilt in-the-ditch between the navy blue square and border.
3. Bind the edges.
4. Draw the moon eye with fabric paint.

Quilt

Dog Days of Summer

Color photo on page 27

The dog days of summer are the hottest days of the year, from early July to the middle of August. Hang the quilt in October as well, to remind us all of Adopt-a-Shelter-Dog Month. These four foundation-pieced pooches, basking in the summer sun, differ only in the shapes of their ears.

Dog Block: 4½" x 6"

Materials: 44"-wide fabric

⅛ yd. each of 4 fabrics for dogs
⅛ yd. each of 4 close-contrasting fabrics for dogs
⅓ yd. for background (includes binding)
13" square of batting
½ yd. for backing
Black embroidery floss
8 black 3mm beads for eyes

Cutting

Note: Cut the binding strips and background pieces from the background fabric first, then use the remainder for foundation piecing.

Fabric	Piece No.	No. of Pieces	Dimensions
Background	1	2	1" x 12½"
	2	1	2½" x 12½"

Assembly

Refer to Foundation Piecing on page 12. Use block designs on pages 107–108. Sections A, B, and C are pieced the same for each of the 4 dogs. Use the appropriate ear sections (D) for each dog.

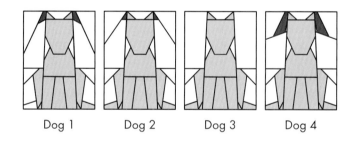

Dog 1 Dog 2 Dog 3 Dog 4

1. Foundation-piece section A through piece A6. The raw edges of A5 and A6 should extend at least as far as the dotted line.

2. Make a paper template of A7; pin on the wrong side of the dog fabric. Cut out, adding a ¼"-wide seam allowance to sides X, Y, and Z, and a more generous seam allowance to the other sides. Press the seam allowances under on sides X, Y, and Z, using the edge of the paper as a guide. Remove the paper.

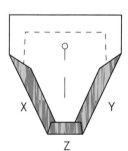

3. Place dog head A7 on foundation-pieced A4, right sides together, centering on line Z as shown; pin in place. Open the folds and machine stitch on the crease of side Z only from fold to fold; backstitch at both ends.

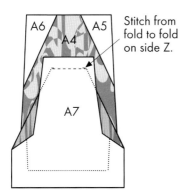

Stitch from fold to fold on side Z.

4. Refold seam allowances on sides X and Y. Flip A7 right side up and press. Blindstitch sides X and Y in place.

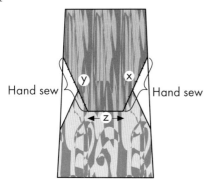

Hand sew

Hand sew

5. Foundation-piece section B and sew to section A.
6. Foundation-piece sections C1–C5 and C1–C5 reversed.
7. Repeat steps 1–6 for the other 3 dogs.
8. For Dog 1, foundation-piece ear sections D1–D3 and D1–D3 reversed. Sew to the hind leg sections, then add to the dog body.

9. Repeat for Dog 2 and Dog 4, using the appropriate ear sections.
10. For Dog 3, sew the single D1 and D1 reversed to the hind leg sections, then add to the dog body.
11. Assemble the dogs and background strips as shown.

Finishing

Refer to pages 16–19 to finish your quilt.

1. Find the center of the quilt top. Using the sun quilt design on page 108, align the center dot on the sun with the quilt center and trace the design on the quilt top.
2. Layer the quilt top with 13" squares of batting and backing. Trim the batting and backing so they extend ¼" beyond the quilt top. Baste.
3. Machine quilt the sun. Stitch around the design 2 or 3 times to make a heavy line. Add beads for eyes and embroider the noses.
4. Bind the edges.

Quilt

County Fair

Color photo on page 28

August and September are months of old-fashioned county fairs and harvest festivals, full of livestock, prize vegetables, and, of course, award-winning quilts.

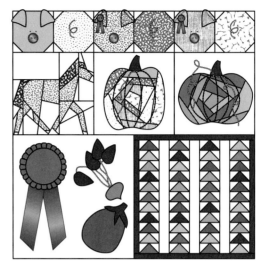

Horse Block: 4"   Pig Block: 2"

Materials: 44"-wide fabric

Assorted scraps of:
- 6 fabrics for pigs
- 2 contrasting fabrics for horse
- orange for pumpkins
- green for vegetable stems and leaves
- purple for eggplant
- red for beet
- blue for ribbon
- several medium to dark fabrics for Flying Geese quilt

¼ yd. for background
13" square of batting
½ yd. for backing
¼ yd. for binding
¼ yd. dark blue ruffle for ribbon
2" scrap of ⅛"-wide dark blue grosgrain ribbon
2" scrap of ⅛"-wide red ribbon for pigs
2 small buttons, ¼" diameter, 1 dark blue and 1 red, for pig ribbons
3 buttons, ½" diameter, with 2 holes for pig noses
Black seed beads or black fabric paint for pig eyes
Green, brown, and assorted embroidery floss (to match pig behinds)

Cutting

Fabric	Piece No.	No. of Pieces	Dimensions
Pig fabrics	1	6*	2½" x 2½"
	T1	12**	
Greens	T4	2	
	T6	1	
	T7	2 + 2r	
Purple	T5	1	
Red	T8	1	
Blue	T9	1	
Flying geese	5	44	1½" x 1"
Background***	2	24	1" x 1"
	3	2	4½" x 4½"
	4	2	6½" x 6½"
	6	44	1¼" x 1¼" ◻
	7	3	1" x 6"
	8	1	6" x 6"

*1 from each fabric
**4 from each of 3 fabrics to match pig faces
***Cut the squares and rectangles from the background fabric first, then use remaining fabric for the foundation-pieced horse.

Assembly

Refer to Foundation Piecing on page 12, and Spiral Crazy Patchwork and Paper-Patch Appliqué on page 14. Use templates and 4" Horse block design on pages 112–13.

Pigs

1. Make 2 ears for each of the 3 pig faces. Sew 2 piece T1 right sides together, leaving the straight edge open. Trim the seam allowance at the point and turn inside out.
2. Speed-piece a background 4 to each bottom corner of a pig 1. Speed-piece a background 4 to each top corner of a pig 1, catching the raw edge of the ears in the seams.

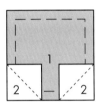 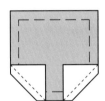 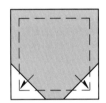

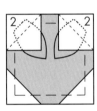 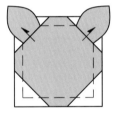 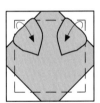

4. Tack the ear tips to the face. Make 3 pig faces.
5. For 3 pig behinds, speed-piece a background 4 to all 4 corners of a pig 1.
6. Sew 6 pigs together in a row, being careful not to catch the ears in the seams.

Horse

Foundation-piece one 4" horse, following assembly steps 1 and 2 on page 54. Trim the horse to 4½" x 4½".

Pumpkins

1. Transfer T2 and T3 to paper for foundation piecing. Cover with scraps of spiral crazy patchwork in orange fabrics.
2. Paper-patch T2 and T3. Paper-patch 2 green stems (T4), turning under sides and narrow top.

3. Appliqué a pumpkin and stem to each background 3, tucking the raw edge of the stem base under the pumpkin.
4. Embroider dark lines on the pumpkins and then embroider the green vines.

Eggplant, Beet, and Blue Ribbon

1. Paper-patch eggplant (T5), eggplant stem (T6), 4 beet leaves (T7, 2 + 2 reversed), and beet (T8).
2. Appliqué eggplant, then eggplant stem to background 4.
3. Appliqué beet leaves and beet to background 4. Embroider green beet stems.
4. For the blue ribbon, paper-patch T9. Cut 2 streamers, each 3½" long, from the dark blue grosgrain ribbon. Tuck ribbon streamers and ruffle under T9 and appliqué T9 to background 4, sewing through the ruffle and the ribbon.

Flying Geese Quilt

1. Foundation-piece 4 Flying Geese strips, using precut rectangles 5 from assorted medium and dark fabrics and background 6 triangles.
2. Sew the Flying Geese strips and background 7 strips together. Refer to the quilt plan.
3. Pin the quilt top and the background 8 square wrong sides together. Quilt straight lines down the centers of the background strips.
4. Bind with 1½" strips of Flying Geese fabric, double folded, to make ¼" finished binding.

Finishing

Refer to pages 16–19 to finish your quilt.

1. Referring to the diagram of the quilt on page 70, sew the sections together, using background 4 in place of the Flying Geese quilt.
2. Layer the quilt top with 13" squares of batting and backing. Trim the batting and backing so they extend ¼" beyond the quilt top. Baste.
3. Quilt around the pumpkins, the beet, and the eggplant.
4. Bind the edges.
5. Embroider the pig tails.
6. Add buttons for pig noses. For pig eyes, sew on black seed beads or paint with fabric paint.
7. For pig ribbons, tack 2 pieces of ⅛"-wide ribbon to a pig ear and sew on a matching button.
8. Tack the Flying Geese quilt in place.

Quilt

Ballooning

Color photo on page 28

Few things are as color-ful as a summer sky full of hot-air balloons. Make yours from geometric prints or from fabrics you construct by foundation piecing and strip piecing.

Hang your quilt to celebrate summer. Or commemorate the first balloon flight (June 5, 1783), the first manned balloon flight (November 21, 1783), or the birthday of Jules Verne (February 8).

Materials: 44"-wide fabric

Scraps of solids and prints for balloons
²/₃ yd. for background (includes binding)
13" square of batting
½ yd. for backing
Embroidery floss in assorted colors

Assembly

Refer to Speed Piecing on page 11, Foundation Piecing on page 12, and Paper-Patch Appliqué on page 14. Use templates below.

1. Prepare the fabrics for balloons (T1), following the directions for making the easter eggs on pages 47–49. For strip-pieced design A (Egg A), cut the top piece 1⅝" x 3" and the bottom piece 3" x 3".
2. Paper-patch the balloons.
3. Cut a 12½" x 12½" square from the background fabric. Arrange the balloons on the background square. Appliqué in place.
4. Embroider the ropes and gondolas.

Finishing

Refer to pages 16–19 to finish your quilt.

1. Layer the quilt top with 13" squares of batting and backing. Trim the batting and backing so they extend ¼" beyond the quilt top. Baste.
2. Quilt around the balloons.
3. Bind the edges.

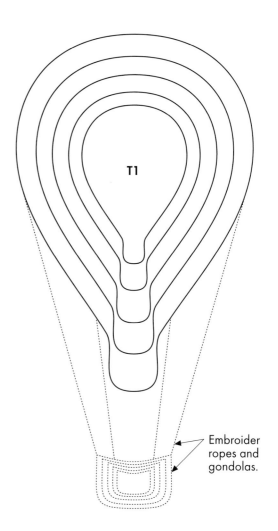

T1

Embroider ropes and gondolas.

Quilt

First Day of School

Color photo on page 28

The first day of school is often the day after Labor Day, which is the first Monday in September. Also hang this quilt during the first full week of May, Teacher Appreciation Week; National Teacher Day is Tuesday of that week.

Look for fun fabrics for the computer screens; good sources are the instructions and diagrams printed on fabric panels. Or type your quilt label on muslin and use it for one or more of the screens.

Materials: 44"-wide fabric

¼ yd. for background
Scraps of:
  dark red for schoolhouse
  dark gray for schoolhouse roof and door
  reds, apple greens, and/or golds for apples
  green for apple leaves
  brown for apple stems
  a variety of solids and/or tone-on-tones for school books
  light grays, browns, greens, and/or blues for computers
  fabrics printed with words or tiny diagrams for computer screens
  black for chalkboard
13" square of batting
½ yd. for backing
¼ yd. for binding
White and black fabric paint for computer and chalkboard details

Cutting

Fabric	Piece No.	No. of Pieces	Dimensions
Background	1	1	1½" x 6½"
	2	1	2" x 6½"
	3	2	1½" x 8½"
	4	1	2½" x 10½"
Apple fabrics	T1	5	
Green	T2	4	
Brown	5	5	½" x 1"
Black	4	1	2½" x 10½"

Assembly

Refer to Foundation Piecing on page 12 and Paper-Patch Appliqué on page 14. Use templates and block designs on pages 114–15.

1. Foundation-piece the schoolhouse. Sew C to B, then B/C to A, then add D and E. Trim to 6½" wide by 6" tall.

2. Add background borders 1, 2, and 3 to the schoolhouse in numerical order. Press the seam allowances toward the border strips. Remove the foundation paper.

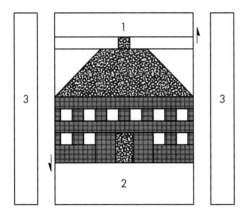

3. Paper-patch appliqué templates T1 and T2.
4. Appliqué the apples to background 4, spacing them evenly along the length of the strip.
5. For each apple stem, fold ¼" under on ends of piece 5 and finger-press. Trim to ¼" wide at bottom, tapering to ½" at top of stem. Appliqué, turning under ⅛" on long edges as you appliqué.

6. Appliqué 3 leaves to apple stems. The last leaf will be appliquéd after the outer borders are added to the schoolhouse. The top apple does not have a leaf.

7. Sew the apple border to the right side of the schoolhouse, aligning the top edges. Begin stitching at the top and stop about 1" from the bottom edge of the schoolhouse unit.

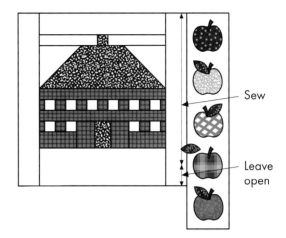

8. Foundation-piece schoolbook sections A, B, and C. To make a short book (pieces B8, B9, and C9), sew a piece of background fabric to the book fabric before adding it to the foundation.
9. Sew the 3 sections together. Trim to 2½" x 10½".
10. Sew the schoolbook border to the top of the schoolhouse.
11. Foundation-piece computer sections A, B, and C. Sew the sections together. Make 5 computers. Trim each to 2½" x 2½".
12. Sew the 5 computers together in a vertical row.
13. Sew the computer border to the left side of the schoolhouse.
14. Sew chalkboard 4 to the bottom of the schoolhouse.
15. Finish the apple border seam.
16. Appliqué the last apple leaf on the schoolhouse/border seam.

Finishing

Refer to pages 16–19 to finish your quilt.
1. Layer the quilt top with 13" squares of batting and backing. Trim the batting and backing so they extend ¼" beyond the quilt top. Baste.
2. Quilt around the schoolhouse.
3. Bind the edges.
4. With black fabric paint, add dots to each computer for dials.
5. With white fabric paint, print letters on the chalkboard border.

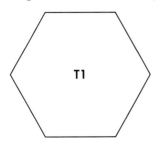

Quilt

Grandparents' Day

Color photo on page 29

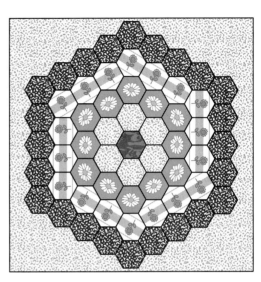

Make a traditional English paper-pieced Grandmother's Flower Garden block to celebrate Grandparents' Day, the first Sunday in September after Labor Day. September 15 is Respect for the Aged Day in Japan, a national holiday.

Use dainty floral prints, or use fabrics that remind you of your own grandparents. Does your grandfather fish, or your grandmother watch birds? Do they love cats, roses, or vacations in Hawaii? With all the novelty prints available today, there are many ways to personalize your quilt.

Materials: 44"-wide fabric

⅛ yd. or scraps of 5 fabrics for block center and 4 rounds
½ yd. for background
13" square of batting
½ yd. for backing
¼ yd. for binding

Cutting

1. Make a hexagon template of T1 (below) from transparent template plastic. Trace and cut 61 hexagons from lightweight cardstock or construction paper.
2. Using the transparent plastic template, cut out fabric hexagons, adding a ¼"-wide seam allowance all around. Center motifs if desired. Cut 1 hexagon for the center, 6 for the first round, 12 for the second round, 18 for the third round, and 24 for the fourth round.
3. Cut a 12½" square from the background fabric.

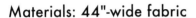

T1

Assembly

Refer to Paper-Patch Appliqué on page 14.

1. Paper-patch each hexagon. Press.
2. Working from the center outward, whipstitch the hexagons together. Place the hexagons right sides together and sew from the wrong side.

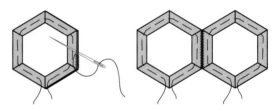

3. When all the hexagons have been joined, press the piece and remove the basting threads and paper.
4. Appliqué the block to the background square.

Finishing

Refer to pages 16–19 to finish your quilt.

1. Layer the quilt top with 13" squares of batting and backing. Trim the batting and backing so they extend ¼" beyond the quilt top. Baste.
2. Quilt around each round of the Grandmother's Flower Garden block.
3. Bind the edges.

Quilt

Falling Leaves

Color photo on page 29

These foundation-pieced leaves can be assembled quickly from bright autumn-colored scraps. In the sample quilt, one fabric is used for each leaf, but you could also mix different shades and prints of the same color, or mix colors in each leaf. The irregular rectangles between the leaves increase the sense of motion.

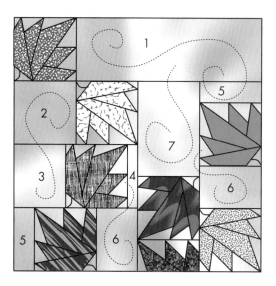

Leaf Block: 3"

Materials: 44"-wide fabric

1/8 yd. each of 8 different autumn colors for leaves
1/4 yd. for background
13" square of batting
1/2 yd. for backing
1/4 yd. for binding
Assorted embroidery floss to match leaves

Cutting

Note: Cut the squares and rectangles from the background fabric first, then use the remaining fabric for the foundation-pieced leaves.

Fabric	Piece No.	No. of Pieces	Dimensions
Background	1	1	3½" x 9½"
	2	1	3½" x 3½"
	3	1	3" x 3½"
	4	1	1" x 3½"
	5	2	1½" x 3½"
	6	2	2½" x 3½"
	7	1	3½" x 5"

Assembly

Refer to Foundation Piecing on page 12. Use block design on page 117.

1. Foundation-piece 8 leaves. Trim each leaf block to 3½" square.

2. From 1 leaf, cut away 1½" as shown, so the remainder measures 2" x 3½".

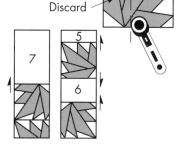

Discard

3. Assemble the leaves and background pieces, following the piecing diagrams. Remove the paper foundations.

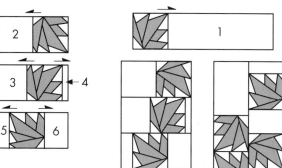

Finishing

Refer to pages 16–19 to finish your quilt.

1. Embroider the leaf stems.
2. Layer the quilt top with 13" squares of batting and backing. Trim the batting and backing so they extend ¼" beyond the quilt top. Baste.
3. Draw wind curls freehand and quilt.
4. Bind the edges.

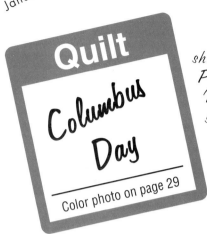

Appliqué Columbus's ships—the Niña, the Pinta, and the Santa María—on a turbulent sea. You can simply appliqué the ships to your background fabric, or you can cut into the fabric and slip the ships under the waves.

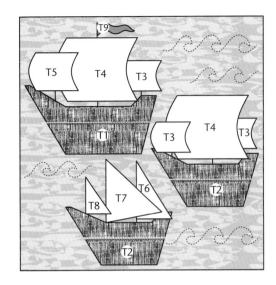

Materials: 44"-wide fabric

⅛ yd. brown print for ships
⅛ yd. or scraps of several white-on-white prints for sails
Scrap of red for pennant
½ yd. for background
13" square of batting
½ yd. for backing
¼ yd. for binding
Red, gold, brown, and black embroidery floss

Cutting

Fabric	Piece No.	No. of Pieces	Dimensions
Brown print	T1	1	
	T2	2	
White prints	T3	3	
	T4	2	
	T5	1	
	T6	1	
	T7	1	
	T8	1	
Red	T9	1	
Background		1	12½" x 12½"

Assembly

Refer to Paper-Patch Appliqué on page 14. Use templates on pages 116–17.

1. Press under ¼" on all the edges of the ships (T1 and T2) and the triangular sails (T6, T7, and T8). (These templates include ¼"-wide seam allowances.) If you can see the background fabric through the sail fabric, use 2 layers of white fabric.

2. Paper-patch the curved sails (T3, T4, and T5) and the pennant (T9). (These templates do not include seam allowances.)

3. Position the tips of the ship prows from the top left corner of the background square according to the measurements below. Pin in place.

Santa María	T1	½" in and 3½" down
Pinta	T2	6¾" in and 6½" down
Niña	T2	2½" in and 9½" down

Note: If you want waves of the background fabric to overlap the bottom edges of the ships, mark the bottom edge of each ship with a pin at each corner, pinning through the background fabric only. Remove the ship and mark the wave line with chalk or a pencil, taking care not to dip below an imaginary line between the two pins. With sharp scissors, cut ⅛" above the drawn line and clip at each end to the pins. Tuck the bottom edge of the ship into the cut. Appliqué the waves to the ship, turning under ⅛" as you sew.

4. Appliqué the ships.

5. Appliqué the sails in place, following the quilt plan.

6. Embroider the masts, centering them below the curved sails and placing the mast along the left edge of triangular sail T6. Extend the mast for the pennant 1" above the center sail of the large ship.

7. Appliqué the pennant.

8. Embroider decorative lines ½" to ¾" from the decks of the ships.

Finishing

Refer to pages 16–19 to finish your quilt.

1. Layer the quilt top with 13" squares of batting and backing. Trim the batting and backing so they extend ¼" beyond the quilt top. Baste.

2. Quilt around each ship. If desired, quilt waves in the spaces between the ships.

3. Bind the edges.

Quilt

Boss's Day

Color photo on page 29

This quilt is for anyone who has ever had to suffer with a real oinker of a boss. It was inspired by a friend of mine who rummaged through everyone's fabric collections a few years ago looking for pig fabrics—to make a pair of shorts for her boss! You can always tell your boss you weren't thinking of him; you were thinking of **his** boss.

Boss's Day is celebrated on October 16. This quilt can also celebrate a Year of the Pig in the Chinese calendar cycle, or the birthday of anyone born in a Year of the Pig. See page 8 for a chart of the animals associated with each year of the twelve-year Chinese cycle.

Note: The quilt plan is merely a guide to show you how I arranged the pieces cut from my fabrics. Since you will be working with a different set of fabrics, cut your pieces based on the sizes of the motifs in your collection and arrange them to fit as instructed on page 79.

Materials: 44"-wide fabric

Scraps of pig-print fabrics
Scraps of 2 pink fabrics for pieced and appliquéd pigs
Assorted pink scraps for coping strips (optional)
Scrap of white for background
13" square of batting
½ yd. for backing
¼ yd. for binding
Pink 2-hole button, ½" in diameter
Pink embroidery floss or pink fabric paint
Black embroidery floss or black fabric paint

Cutting

Fabric	Piece No.	No. of Pieces	Dimensions
Pink 1	1	1	2½" x 2½"
(pieced pig)	T1	4	
Pink 2	T2	1	
(appliquéd pig)	T3	1	
	3	3	¾" x ⅞"
Background	2	4	1" x 1"
	4	1	2½" x 3½"

Assembly

Refer to Paper-Patch Appliqué on page 14. Use templates on page 114.

1. Following the instructions on page 71, make 1 pig face, using pink 1 and T1, and background 2.

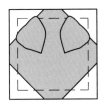

2. For the appliqué pig, paper-patch templates T2 and T3. Press under ¼" on the short sides and one long side on each pink 3.

3. Pin body (T2) to background 4. Pin the snout and legs in place. Appliqué snout and legs, then body and ear.

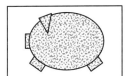

4. Make a list of your pig fabrics and the optimum finished size of each pig cutout. Starting with the largest cutouts, sketch your quilt on graph paper. Adjust the sizes of the cutouts as necessary.
5. Next to each pig fabric, list the cutting measurements for each piece. Cut out the pigs.
6. Sew pieces together to make a 12½" square. Before you sew, analyze your sketch and make an assembly plan that avoids inset seams (internal corners) as much as possible.

Hint

You may find it easier to fit the pieces together if you add coping strips to some of the motifs. These could match the background of the motif or could contrast to complement the pig motifs. Add pink strips or add a strip to which you've added an "oink" in fabric paint, ink, or embroidery floss.

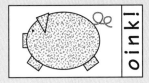

Finishing

Refer to pages 16–19 to finish your quilt.

1. Layer the quilt top with 13" squares of batting and backing. Trim the batting and backing so they extend ¼" beyond the quilt top. Baste.
2. Quilt around some of the pigs by hand or machine.
3. Bind the edges.
4. Add a button for the pieced pig's nose; glue or sew in place.
5. Paint or embroider a pink curled tail on the appliquéd pig.
6. Paint or embroider black eyes on the pieced and appliquéd pigs.

Quilt

Happy Halloween

Color photo on page 30

Halloween, the night of October 31, is a time to celebrate ghosts, ghouls, and all things creepy and crawly. In keeping with the holiday, this jack-o'-lantern quilt is embellished with a machine-embroidered spider web and two big rubber spiders.

Materials: 44"-wide fabric

1/8 yd. orange for pumpkin
Scrap of green for stem
1/3 yd. black for background (includes binding)
13" square of batting
1/2 yd. for backing
White or silver thread for machine embroidery
2 rubber spiders, about 3" in diameter
White glue

Cutting

Note: The squares and rectangles you cut may not look like the corresponding pieces in the block diagram because the diagonals are speed-pieced. The diagram shows you the location of each piece, not necessarily its actual shape.

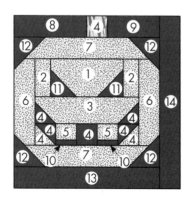

Fabric	Piece No.	Pieces	Dimensions
Orange	1	1	2¼" x 4"
	2	2	1¼" x 2¼"
	3	1	1¾" x 5½"
	4	2	1½" x 1½"
	5	2	1¼" x 1½"
	6	2	1½" x 4½"
	7	2	1½" x 7½"
Green	4	1	1½" x 1½"
Black	4	5	1½" x 1½"
	8	1	1½" x 4"
	9	1	1½" x 3"
	10	2	½" x 1½"
	11	2	1¾" x 1¾"
	12	4	2" x 2"
	13	1	1½" x 7½"
	14	1	1½" x 8½"
	15	1	4½" x 8½"
	16	1	4½" x 12½"

Assembly

1. Speed-piece a black 11 to opposite ends of an orange 1. Sew an orange 2 to opposite ends.

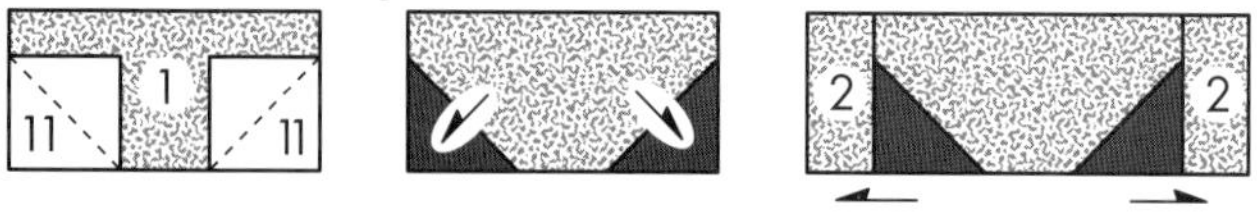

2. Speed-piece a black 4 to opposite ends of an orange 3.

3. Sew a black 10 to the long side of each orange 5. Join these with three black 4 pieces, alternating the pieces as shown. Speed-piece an orange 4 to opposite ends.

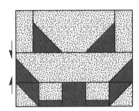

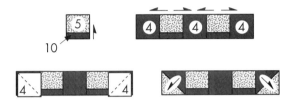

4. Sew the 3 face pieces together.

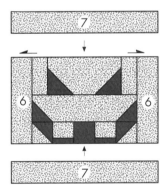

5. Sew an orange 6 to opposite sides of the face. Sew an orange 7 to the top and bottom of the face.

6. Speed-piece a black 12 to each corner of the pumpkin face.

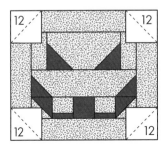

7. Sew black 8 and 9 to opposite sides of green 4. Join this to the top of the pumpkin.

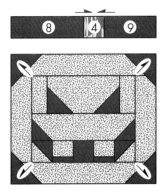

8. Sew black 13 to the bottom of the pumpkin.
9. Sew black 14 to the right side, black 15 to the left side, and black 16 to the top of the pumpkin. Refer to the quilt plan.

Finishing

Refer to pages 16–19 to finish your quilt.

1. Draw the spider web lines with a chalk marker or silver pencil. Using a ruler, draw 8½" straight lines first, radiating from the upper left corner of the quilt top, then draw the curved connecting lines freehand. Use the quilt plan and color photograph of the quilt as guides, but don't worry about being precise; real spider webs are not exactly symmetrical. Machine stitch on the drawn lines with white or silver machine-embroidery thread.
2. Layer the quilt top with 13" squares of batting and backing. Trim the batting and backing so they extend ¼" beyond the quilt top. Baste.
3. Quilt around the pumpkin.
4. Bind the edges. Before turning the binding to the back and sewing it down, thread a needle with a 16" piece of white or silver machine-embroidery thread and pull it through the binding seam. Make a knot to secure it.

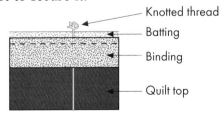

5. Glue 1 spider to the web. Tie the end of the thread around the other spider. Where it is tied around the spider, color the thread black with a felt pen so it doesn't show.

Quilt

Veterans Day

Color photo on page 30

Following World War I, on Veterans Day (formerly Armistice Day), families hung stars in their windows in recognition of family members in military service: blue stars for those who served in wartime, and gold stars for those who gave their lives.

These irregular stars are foundation-pieced in three sections; no templates are required. Rotate the stars and reverse one or two so each star looks different; or draw your own stars so all four are quite different (see the Hint box below right).

Materials: 44"-wide fabric

¼ yd. gold for stars and border
¼ yd. navy blue for stars and binding
⅛ yd. for background
13" square of batting
½ yd. for backing

Cutting

Note: First cut the strips for the borders from the gold fabric, and for the binding from the navy blue fabric, then use the remaining fabric for the stars.

Fabric		No. of Pieces	Dimensions
Gold	top/bottom borders	2	1½" x 10½"
	side borders	2	1½" x 12½"

Assembly

Refer to Foundation Piecing on page 12. Use block design on page 117.

1. Foundation-piece 4 stars (2 gold and 2 navy blue, reversing one or two if desired). For each star, foundation-piece sections A, B, and C in numerical order, then join the sections in order: A to B, then A/B to C.

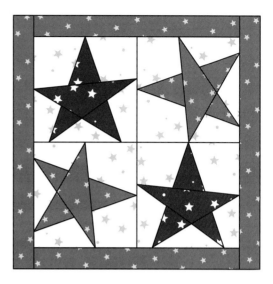

Star Block: 5"

2. Sew the 4 stars together, alternating the colors and rotating the stars.
3. Add the top and bottom borders and press, then add the side borders and press.

Finishing

Refer to pages 16–19 to finish your quilt.

1. Layer the quilt top with 13" squares of batting and backing. Trim the batting and backing so they extend ¼" beyond the quilt top. Baste.
2. Quilt around each star.
3. Bind the edges.

Hint

Designing Irregular Five-Pointed Stars

Design your own irregular five-pointed stars, in any size. Draw a square on graph paper the size of the finished star. Mark five points on the square, approximately equal distances apart. Draw lines connecting every other mark. Divide your stars into three sections for foundation piecing.

The more unequal the distances between the marks, the more irregular the star.

Quilt

Thanksgiving

Color photo on page 30

Thanksgiving was the first national holiday declared by presidential proclamation—by President George Washington in 1782. It is a day set aside for public thanksgiving for our blessings. It corresponds to harvest festivals celebrated for thousands of years, including the Jewish harvest festival Sukkot, which falls in September or October. Paper-patch appliqué this bounty of vegetables, or if you are in a hurry, fuse the design. Look for a narrow-stripe fabric for the cornucopia, and a variety of purples for the grapes.

Materials: 44"-wide fabric

¼ yd. orange for pumpkin
¼ yd. narrow stripe for cornucopia
Scrap of dark fabric for cornucopia rim
Assorted scraps of reds, greens, and purples for fruits and vegetables
⅛ yd. of ¼" yellow check for corn
½ yd. for background
13" square of batting
½ yd. for backing
¼ yd. for binding
Brown and green embroidery floss

Cutting

Fabric	Piece No.	No. of Pieces	Dimensions
Orange	T2	1	
Cornucopia	T3	1	
Cornucopia rim	T4	1	
Apple red 1	T5	1	
Apple red 2	T6	1	
Yellow check	T9	2	

continued next column

Fabric	Piece No.	No. of Pieces	Dimensions
Green	T1	1	
	T7	1	
	T8	2	
	T10	1	
	T11	1 + 1r	
Asst. purples	T12	20	
Asst. reds	T13	1 + 1r	
	T14	1	
	T15	2 + 1r	
	T16	1	
Background		1	12½" x 12½"

Assembly

Refer to Paper-Patch Appliqué on page 14. Use templates on pages 118–20.

1. Paper-patch all pieces except the cornucopia (T3).
2. To make the cornucopia, take 4 darts by folding on the solid lines, right sides together, and matching the dotted lines. Sew on the dotted lines. Press all the darts to one side. Baste under ¼" all around the cornucopia and press.
3. Appliqué pieces to the background square in the following order: pumpkin stem (T1), pumpkin (T2), cornucopia (T3), cornucopia rim (T4), apple (T5), apple (T6), apple leaf (T7), corn stem (T8), corn (T9), husk (T11r), corn stem (T8), corn (T9), husk (T10), husk (T11), and grapes (T12).

4. To make the chili pepper braid, cut 3 pieces of 6-strand brown embroidery floss, each 16" long. Make a bundle of the strands and fold the bundle in half. Pin the folded end to your ironing board to anchor it and braid the strands in 3 bundles of 12 strands each. Trim the braid to 5" long. Tack the top of the braid to the background square with the fold extending slightly over the top raw edge; tack the bottom end of the braid as well, but leave the rest free so some of the peppers can be slipped under it.

5. Appliqué the peppers (T13–T16), sewing some above the braid and slipping some under it. The last pepper (T16) should cover the bottom cut edge of the braid.

6. Embroider the apple stems, the grape stem, the grape tendrils, and the pumpkin tendrils.

Finishing

Refer to pages 16–19 to finish your quilt.

1. Layer the quilt top with 13" squares of batting and backing. Trim the batting and backing so they extend ¼" beyond the quilt top. Baste.

2. Quilt around the pumpkin and stem, the cornucopia, the apples, and the ears of corn. Referring to pumpkin template (T1), quilt the pumpkin lines with black thread.

3. With matching yellow thread or invisible nylon thread, take a backstitch at each corner of the ¼" checks on the ears of corn. Stitch through the top, batting, and backing, so there are short stitches on the front of the quilt and long stitches on the back.

4. Bind the edges.

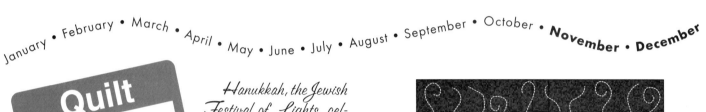

January • February • March • April • May • June • July • August • September • October • **November** • **December**

Quilt

Hanukkah

Color photo on page 30

Hanukkah, the Jewish Festival of Lights, celebrates the recapture from enemies and cleansing of the temple in Jerusalem. A lamp was lit on the altar that had been dark for many years. Although there was only a small amount of oil, the temple lamp burned for eight days. The festival celebrating this miracle lasts for eight days; each day, another of the eight candles of the menorah is lit from the ninth candle.

This is a simple pieced menorah with foundation-pieced candle flames. Menorah candles can be all one color or different colors, but are seldom white. Here, striped fabrics are cut on the diagonal to imitate candles with spiral grooves. If you use a metallic fabric for the candle stand, be careful when pressing it; some metallics melt easily.

Materials: 44"-wide fabric

⅛ yd. each of 5 different fabrics for candles*
Scrap of yellow for candle flames
⅛ yd. silver metallic fabric for candle stand
⅓ yd. for background (includes binding)
13" square of batting
½ yd. for backing

*You will need ¼ yd. of each fabric if you plan to cut the candles on the diagonal.

Cutting

Fabric	Piece No.	No. of Pieces	Dimensions
Candles	1	2 each from 4 fabrics; 1 from 5th fabric	1¼" x 6½"
Background	2	8	1" x 8"
	3	2	1⅛" x 8"
	4	2	3" x 6⅛"
	5	1	1¼" x 2"
	9	2	2" x 5½"
Silver	6	1	1¼" x 1½"
	7	1	1" x 12½"
	8	1	2" x 2½"

Assembly

Refer to Foundation Piecing on page 12.

1. Using the block design below, foundation-piece 9 candle flames. Make 5 as illustrated and 4 reversed.

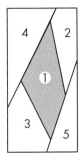

Block design

2. Sew a flame to the end of each candle 1. Sew the 4 reversed flames to the candles on the right of the center candle.

3. Refer to the piecing diagram below as you assemble the pieces. Sew the background 2 pieces between the candles as shown. Sew a background 3 to the inner edge of each group of 4 candles, next to the center candle. Press all seams toward the background fabric.

4. Sew a background 4 to the top of each group of 4 candles.

5. Sew silver 6 to the base of the remaining candle. Sew background 5 to the top of the candle.

6. Join the left and right candle units to the center candle.

7. Sew silver 7 to the bottom of the candles.

8. Sew a background 9 to the short sides of silver 8 to make the menorah base; add to the bottom of silver 7.

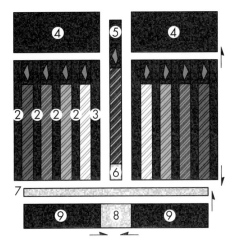

Finishing

Refer to pages 16–19 to finish your quilt.

1. Layer the quilt top with 13" squares of batting and backing. Trim the batting and backing so they extend ¼" beyond the quilt top. Baste.

2. Quilt up the center of each strip between the candles. Above the flames, turn the lines into freehand smoke curls. Quilt around the menorah base.

3. Bind the edges.

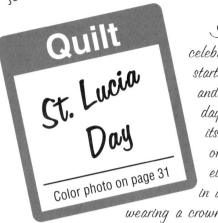

Quilt

St. Lucia Day

Color photo on page 31

In Sweden, the celebration of Christmas starts on St. Lucia Day and continues for twelve days until Christmas day itself. On the morning of December 13, the eldest daughter, dressed in a long white robe and wearing a crown of fir branches and candles, delivers breakfast to the other members of the household, starting twelve days of feasting and celebrating.

In this appliquéd and embroidered quilt, the St. Lucia crown is on a background of blue and is bound with yellow, the colors of Sweden's flag.

Materials: 44"-wide fabric

⅛ yd. white for candles
Scrap of yellow for candle flame
⅓ yd. for background
¼ yd. for border
13" square of batting
½ yd. for backing
¼ yd. for binding (includes candle flames)
#5 green pearl cotton or embroidery floss

Cutting

Fabric	Piece No.	No. of Pieces	Dimensions
White		4	⅞" x 4¾"
		3	⅞" x 4¼"
Yellow	T1	4	
	T2	3	
Background			10" x 10"
Border	sides	2	2" x 9½"
	top/bottom	2	2" x 12½"

Assembly

Refer to Paper-Patch Appliqué on page 14. Use templates on page 121.

1. Press under ¼" on the 2 long edges and bottom of the white candle strips. Press the top of the candle at an angle. Using the placement diagram on page 121, position the candles on the 10" background square with the 4 longer candles in front. Appliqué in place.

2. Paper-patch candle flames (T1 and T2). Appliqué in place above the candles.

3. With the piece in an embroidery frame or hoop, embroider fir branches using pearl cotton or 6 strands of embroidery floss. Make your stitches irregular, as shown below. Be careful not to pull the stitches too tight. Stitch the spines of the branches and a few needles for each, all around the circle, then go back and fill in the needles with random stitches. Cover the bases of the candles.

4. Press and trim the background square to 9½" x 9½".

5. Add the border strips to the sides, then to the top and bottom. The sample quilt has a mitered border, to take advantage of the striped print.

Finishing

Refer to pages 16–19 to finish your quilt.

1. Layer the quilt top with 13" squares of batting and backing. Trim the batting and backing so they extend ¼" beyond the quilt top. Baste.

2. Quilt a halo around each candle flame and quilt just inside the border.

3. Bind the edges.

Shadow appliqué makes an unusually delicate Christmas wall hanging. Choose vivid solids for the holly leaves and bow so they will show through the organdy covering.

Color photo on page 31
Variation on page 95

Materials: 44"-wide fabric

⅛ yd. green solid for holly leaves
¼ yd. red solid for bow
½ yd. fabric for background (includes backing and binding)
½ yd. organdy or cotton voile for block covering
13" square of batting
Approximately 12" square of fusible web
Spray glitter (optional)

Caution: Do not press organdy with a hot iron.

Cutting

Fabric	Piece No.	No. of Pieces	Dimensions
Background		1	12½" x 12½"
Organdy		1	12½" x 12½"

Assembly

Refer to Fusible Appliqué on page 15. Use templates on page 122.

1. Trace 21 holly leaves (T1) and the pieces for the bow (T2–T6) onto the paper side of the fusible web. Reverse 6 of the leaves.
2. Following package directions, fuse the web to the wrong side of the holly and bow fabrics. Cut out leaves and bow. Peel off the paper backs.
3. Working on your ironing board and referring to the quilt plan, arrange the holly leaves on your background fabric in a wreath, 2 leaves wide.

Notice that the wreath sits a little high on the square so there is room for the bow to hang below it. Lay some of the leaves at angles so the wreath looks graceful and not rigid. Keep overlaps to a minimum because they will be hard to quilt through later.

4. Position the bow pieces to be sure you left room for the bow.
5. Remove the bow pieces and, following package directions, fuse the leaves to the background fabric.
6. Add the bow pieces in numerical order. Fuse in place.

Finishing

Refer to pages 16–19 to finish your quilt.

1. Layer the organdy, quilt top, and 13" squares of batting and backing. Trim the batting and backing so they extend ¼" beyond the quilt top. Baste.
2. Quilt around each leaf and around each part of the bow.
3. Bind the edges with a strip of background covered by an equal-sized strip of organdy. To avoid seams in the organdy, which will be very visible, bind the 4 sides separately rather than using one long binding strip (see "Straight-Corner Binding" on page 18).
4. Add spray glitter if desired.

Quilt

Snow Flurries

Color photo on page 31

This quilt combines several needle crafts: the snowflakes are crocheted, appliquéd, quilted, and beaded. Assemble your own collection of snowflakes and scatter them on a night sky. Hang the quilt to celebrate the beauty of winter, as well as local winter carnivals or snowfests.

Materials: 44"-wide fabric

Assorted scraps of white for snowflakes
1/3 yd. for background (includes binding)
13" square of batting
1/2 yd. for backing
Crocheted snowflakes
Metallic thread
Snowflake sequins
Silver rocaille and bugle beads

Assembly

Refer to Fusible Appliqué on page 15 and Beading on page 19. Use templates on page 123.

Scatter snowflakes as desired on a 12½" x 12½" square of background fabric.

Crocheted snowflakes: Use commercial patterns to make snowflakes in different sizes, or purchase snowflakes. To stiffen snowflakes, soak in a solution of 1 part white glue to 10 parts water. Wring out. Cover one side of a corrugated cardboard box with plastic film or waxed paper. Stretch each snowflake, pin in place, and allow to dry. Sew snowflakes to the background fabric with a few anchoring stitches. Use regular white sewing thread or clear nylon thread. Decorate with beads or pearls if desired.

Appliquéd snowflakes: Trace snowflakes T1, T2, T3, and T4 on the paper side of fusible web and fuse to the wrong side of the white fabric. Cut out carefully and fuse to the background fabric.

Beaded snowflakes: Follow the beading designs on page 123 or create your own.

Finishing

Refer to pages 16–19 to finish your quilt.

1. Layer the quilt top with 13" squares of batting and backing. Trim the batting and backing so they extend ¼" beyond the quilt top. Baste.
2. Quilt snowflakes with metallic thread. Quilt around appliquéd and crocheted snowflakes as desired.
3. Bind the edges.
4. Embellish with plastic snowflake sequins. Secure each one with a bead in the center.

Quilt

Checkered Border Quilt

Color photos on page 32
Quilt size: 18" x 18"

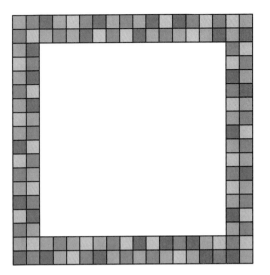

This quilt and its companion, the Accordian-Pleat Border Quilt on page 90, have a space in the center where you can hang your 12" holiday quilts, changing the small quilt with the holidays and seasons.

The multicolored squares and muslin center of this border quilt will go with a number of quilts. This one is so simple to make that you could create others in different color combinations: red, white, and blue for the patriotic-holiday quilts, for example. Or plan your border quilt to match the decor of the room where you'll hang the quilts and choose fabrics for the 12" quilts to match the border quilt.

Attach small squares of Velcro® to the border quilt and the corners of the 12" quilts. Or, since the quilts are so small, you could even attach them with straight pins from the back of the border quilt through the back and batting of the holiday quilt.

Materials: 44"-wide fabric

Scraps of 10 or more fabrics for pieced border
½ yd. background for center panel
19" square of batting
⅔ yd. for backing
¼ yd. for binding
4" of ⅞"-wide, sew-on Velcro tape

Cutting

Fabric	Piece No.	No. of Pieces	Dimensions
Asst. scraps	1	128	1½" x 1½"
Background	2	1	14½" x 14½"

Assembly

1. For the side borders, join 14 of the 1½" squares to make 1 row. Make 4 rows. Sew 2 rows of squares together to make each side border. Sew these to the sides of the center panel.

2. For the top and bottom borders, join 18 squares to make 1 row. Make 4 rows. Sew 2 rows together to make each of the top and bottom borders. Sew these to the top and bottom of the center panel.

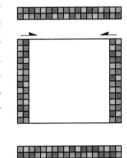

Finishing

Refer to pages 16–19 to finish your quilt.

1. Layer the quilt top with 19" squares of batting and backing. Trim the batting and backing so they extend ¼" beyond the quilt top. Baste.

2. Quilt in-the-ditch around the edge of the center panel. Quilt the center panel in a crosshatch or ornamental design within 1" of the edges; the center quilting should not show when a quilt is attached.

3. Bind the edges.

4. Cut the Velcro into 4 squares. Hand sew the squares 1" in from the border.

Quilt

Accordian-Pleat Border Quilt

Color photos on page 32
Quilt size: 24½" X 24½"

This speed-pieced border takes a little time but is well worth the effort. Select your fabrics carefully. In addition to the background, you will need four fabrics for the border design: a light and a dark version of color A, and a light and a dark version of color B. To maintain the crisp edges of the design and sustain the three-dimensional optical illusion, select solid colors or tone-on-tone fabrics.

Color Key

Light A   Light B   Background

Dark A   Dark B

Materials: 44"-wide fabric

½ yd. light A for strip units (includes binding)
¼ yd. dark A for strip units (includes inner border)
⅛ yd. light B for strip units
⅛ yd. dark B for strip units
¾ yd. for background (includes center panel)
25" square of batting
¾ yd. for backing
4" of ⅞"-wide, sew-on Velcro tape

Cutting

Fabric	Piece No.	No. of Pieces	Dimensions
Light A		2	1½" x 42"
Dark A		2	1½" x 42"
Light B		2	1½" x 42"
Dark B		2	1½" x 42"
Background		1	14½" x 14½"
		4	1½" x 42"
	1	4	2" x 2" ◻
	2	4	2½" x 2½" ◻
Inner Borders	sides	2	1½" x 14½"
	top/bottom	2	1½" x 16½"

Assembly

Note: The directions are easier to follow if you match your fabrics to the illustrations all the way through. Tape snips of your five fabrics next to the color key for reference.

1. Sew the strips together to make strip units I and II, offsetting the ends of each strip 1" as shown below. Make 2 of each strip unit (4 total). Press.

2. Layer a dark strip unit on top of a light strip unit, right sides together, matching the ends and long edges. Trim one end at a 45° angle. (Find the angle on your rotary ruler or use a Bias Square.) Make 1½"-wide crosscuts, maintaining this 45° angle. Cut 18 segments (36 total) from each pair of layered strip units. Keep the pairs of segments together as you cut them, ready for stitching.

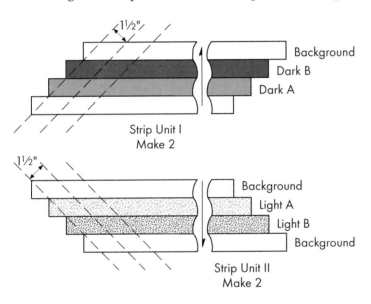

Strip Unit I
Make 2

Strip Unit II
Make 2

3. Sew the segments together in light/dark pairs exactly as shown.

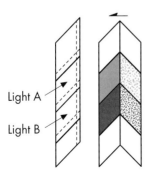

4. For each side of the quilt, stitch 8 pairs together (16 segments). Trim both sides as shown, leaving a ¼"-wide seam allowance beyond the outer points of the design.

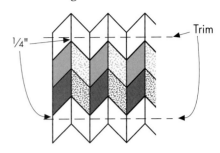

5. Use the remaining 8 pairs of segments to make 4 corner blocks. From 4 of the pairs, remove and discard the background diamond next to the fabric B diamond. From the remaining 4 pairs, remove and discard both the background and the fabric B diamonds.

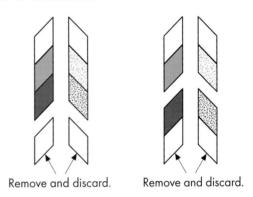

Remove and discard.   Remove and discard.

6. To each of 4 identical small dark fragments, add a background triangle 1 and triangle 2 as shown. Repeat this, only reversed, with the remaining identical small light fragments.

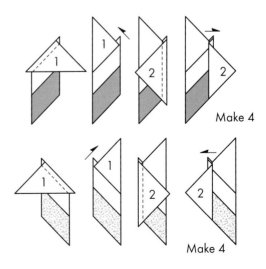

Make 4

Make 4

7. Sew the remaining large segments to the corner units as shown: the large light segment to the small dark unit (shown on the right), and the large dark segment to the small light unit (shown on the left).

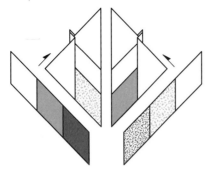

8. Sew the 2 halves together to complete the corner block.

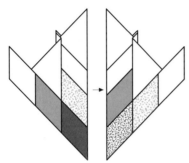

9. Sew the inner side borders to the center panel and press. Then add the inner top and bottom borders and press.
10. Sew 2 pieced border strips to the sides of the center panel.

11. Sew the corner blocks to opposite ends of the 2 remaining pieced border strips. Press the seam allowances toward the corner blocks. Trim the outside edges of the corner blocks even with the border strips. Add the pieced border strips with corner blocks to the top and bottom of the center panel.

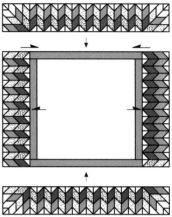

Finishing

Refer to pages 16–19 to finish your quilt.

1. Layer the quilt top with 25" squares of batting and backing. Trim the batting and backing so they extend ¼" beyond the quilt top. Baste.
2. Quilt in-the-ditch on both sides of the inner border. Quilt the center panel in a crosshatch or ornamental design within 1" of the edges; the center quilting should not show when a quilt is attached.
3. Bind the edges.
4. Cut the Velcro into 4 squares. Hand sew the squares to the 4 corners of the center panel, 1" in from the inner border.

Idea Gallery

The quilts in this gallery are all variations of the designs in this book. A few are examples of the designs in other fabrics and colors. Most are larger than the 12" quilts on which the book is based. Individual instructions for these quilts are not provided.

"Springtime in Seattle," shown below, is an example of how the "April Showers" design (page 23) was used to make a large quilt. The umbrellas were assembled in several color combinations and sprinkled over one large piece of a lovely floral print.

I made all of the original quilts 12" square, partly as a challenge to see if I could do it and partly so the designs could be combined in a sampler quilt, which I never made. You may want to combine several of the 12" blocks in one quilt. A four-block quilt could represent the four seasons, or you could make a red, white, and blue quilt from the patriotic designs—by themselves or with alternate star blocks.

There are many ways to use the smaller designs in the book. "SizzleCats" (page 96) has the same number of Cat blocks as the 12" square sample (page 25), but a different setting and a wide border in a vivid print enhance the design. There are four children and grandchildren in my family, so my "Mother's Day" quilt has four blocks; if you have fifteen altogether, you could make a sixteen-block wall hanging and devote the sixteenth block to an embroidered or inked family tree.

Remember that any foundation-pieced design is easy to enlarge or reduce to any size; just take it to your local photocopy shop. "Fire Leaves," in vivid reds and black (page 96), is an expanded version of the 12" "Falling Leaves" quilt (page 29), but it uses the same 3" foundation-pieced leaf. A 6" version of the leaf would make a lovely lap or bed quilt.

Springtime in Seattle ➤
by Virginia Morrison, 1995, Seattle, Washington, 42½" x 61½". Colorful umbrellas seem to drift over a field of flowers in this springtime fantasy.

Dublin Derby by Virginia Morrison, 1995, Seattle, Washington, 51½" x 51½". Trotting horses are the alternate blocks in a variation of the traditional Irish Chain design.

Parade to the Post by Janet Kime, 1995, Vashon Island, Washington, 12" x 12". "Dapples and grays, pintos and bays . . ."—all the pretty horses trotting by in line. ▼

Year of the Horse by Janet Kime, 1995, Vashon Island, Washington, 12" x 12". Novelty-print horses are gathered together to celebrate the Chinese Year of the Horse.

◄ **Year of the Rabbit** by Janet Kime, 1995, Vashon Island, Washington, 20" x 20". Easter bunnies, country bunnies, yo-yo bunnies, even bunny slippers—celebrate the Year of the Rabbit in the twelve-year cycle of the Chinese calendar. Owned by Virginia Morrison.

Family Trees by Janet Kime, 1995, Vashon Island, ► Washington, 12" x 12". Each Christmas tree is decorated with charms that reflect the hobbies of a family member. Owned by Donna Klemka.

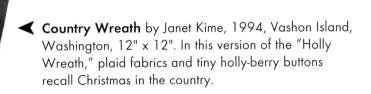

◄ **Country Wreath** by Janet Kime, 1994, Vashon Island, Washington, 12" x 12". In this version of the "Holly Wreath," plaid fabrics and tiny holly-berry buttons recall Christmas in the country.

◄ **Fire Leaves** by Joel T. Patz, 1995, Seattle, Washington, 21" x 27½". Vivid leaves drift over a black background in this wall quilt.

SizzleCats by Janet Kime, 1995, ► Vashon Island, Washington, 15¼" x 25¾". Bright foundation-pieced cats are surrounded by a sizzling border.

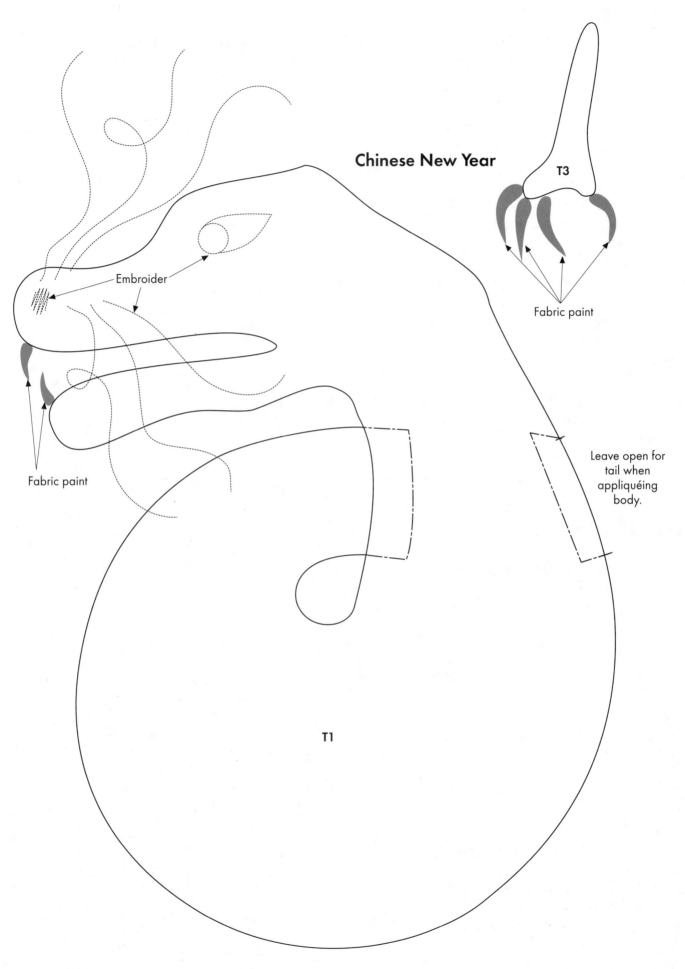

Chinese New Year

T3

Fabric paint

Embroider

Fabric paint

Leave open for
tail when
appliquéing
body.

T1

Chinese New Year

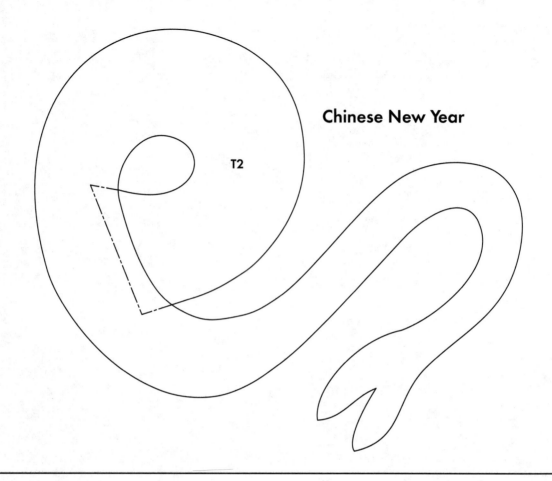

T2

Martin Luther King, Jr. Day

Valentine's Day

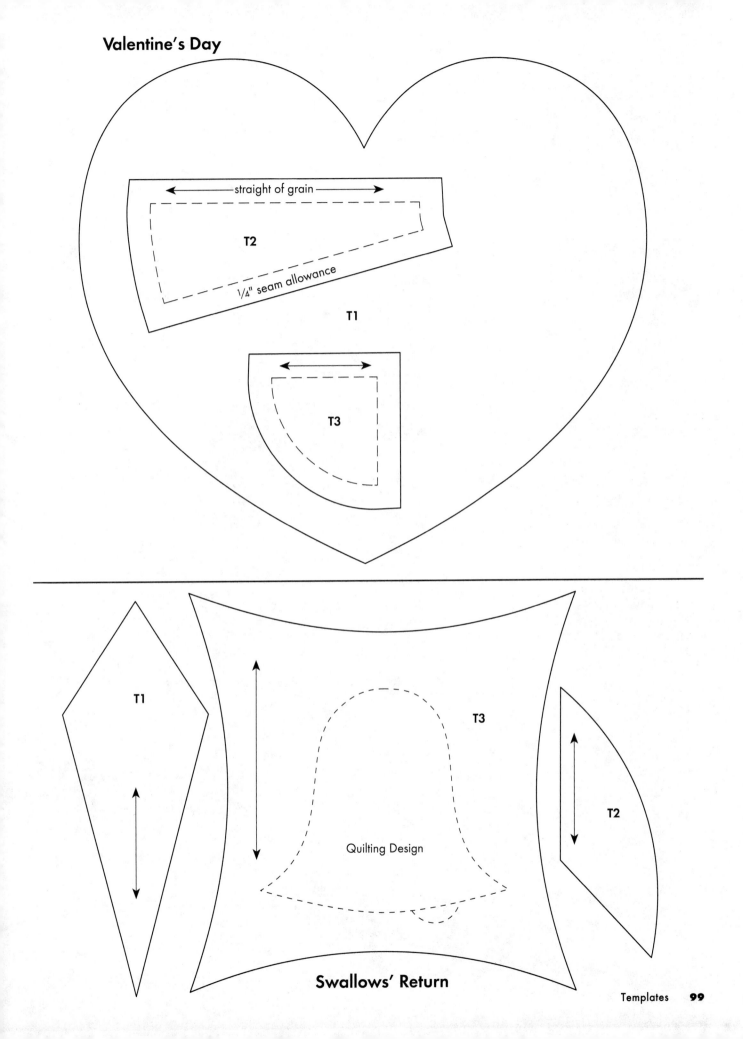

straight of grain

T2

1/4" seam allowance

T1

T3

T1

T3

Quilting Design

T2

Swallows' Return

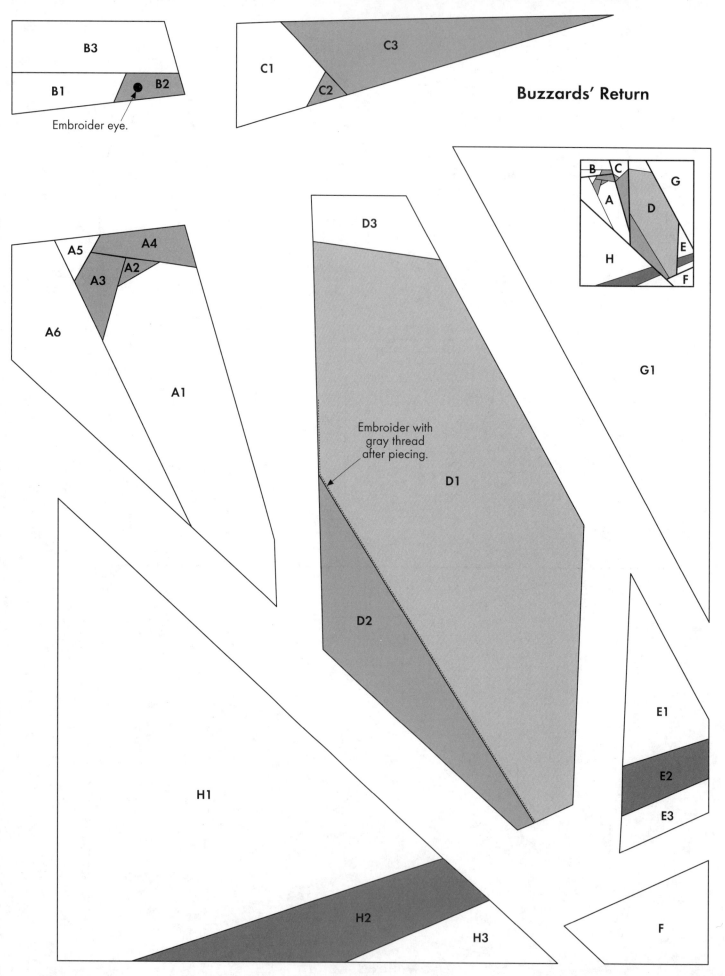

B3

B1

B2

Embroider eye.

C1

C2

C3

Buzzards' Return

B C

A D G

H E

F

A5

A4

A3 A2

A6

A1

D3

G1

Embroider with
gray thread
after piecing.

D1

D2

E1

E2

E3

H1

F

H2

H3

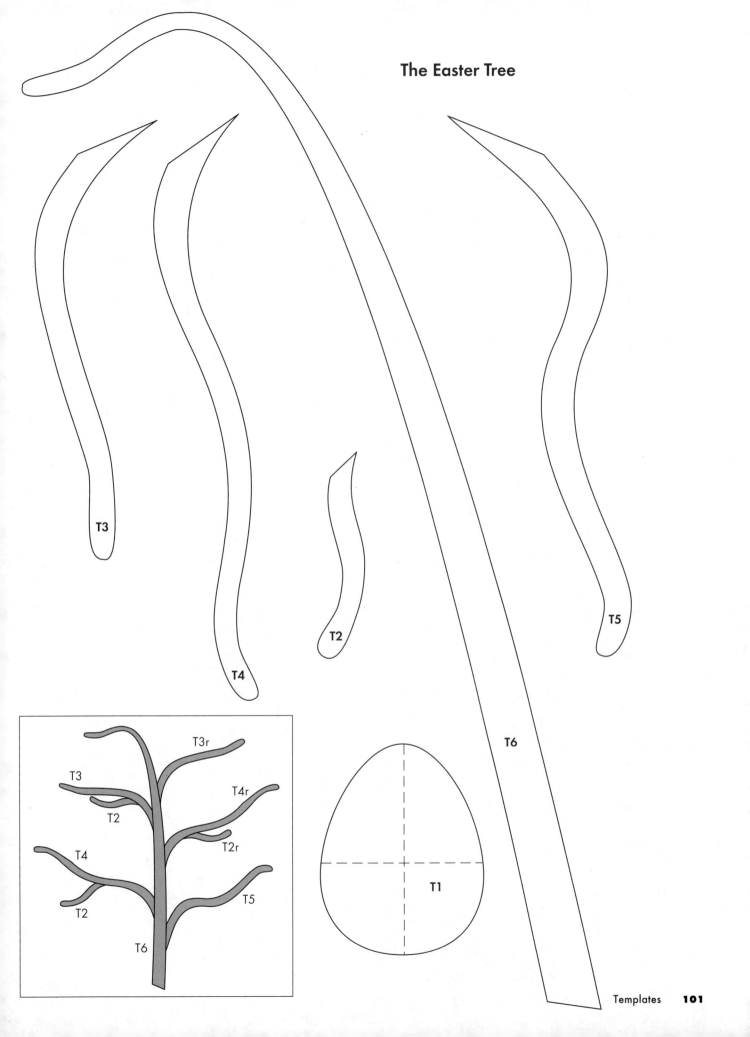

The Easter Tree

T3

T4

T2

T5

T6

T3r

T3

T4r

T2

T2r

T4

T5

T2

T6

T1

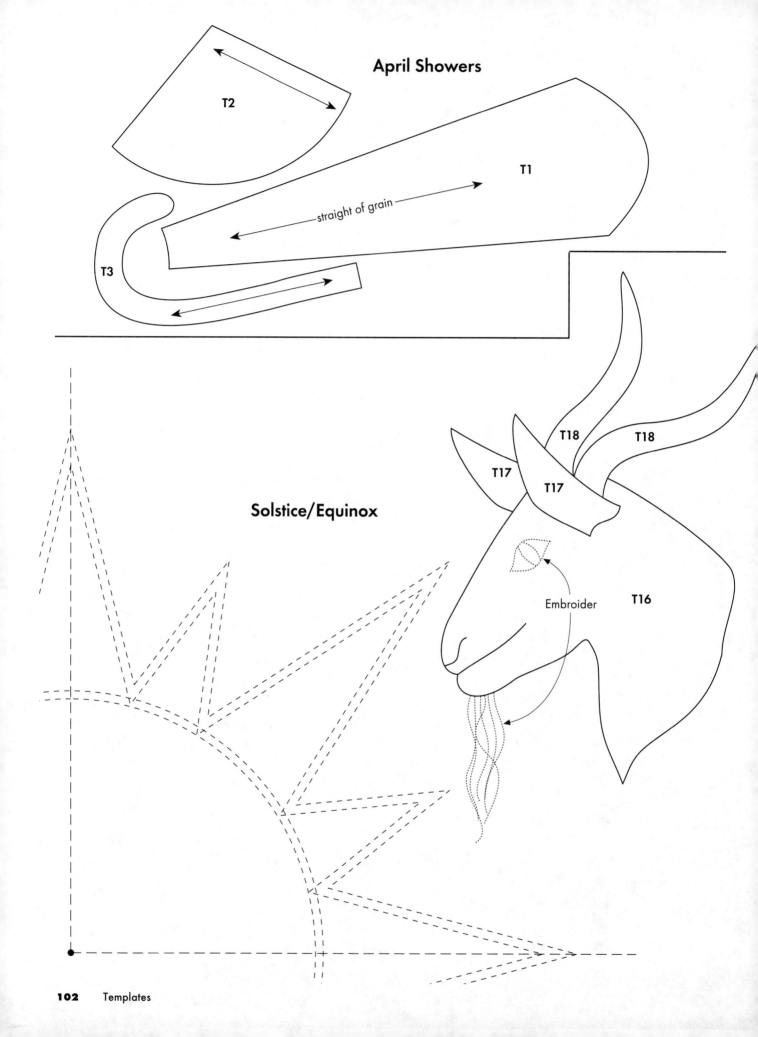

April Showers

T2

T1

straight of grain

T3

Solstice/Equinox

T18

T18

T17

T17

T16

Embroider

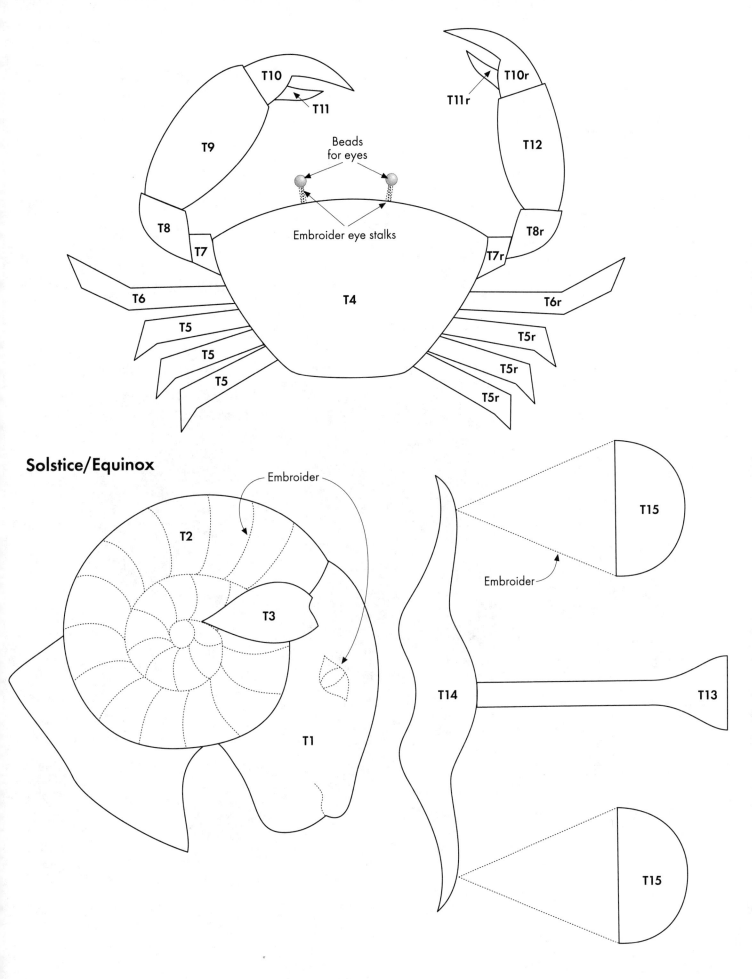

Beads
for eyes

Embroider eye stalks

Solstice/Equinox

Embroider

Embroider

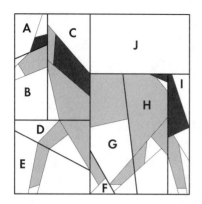

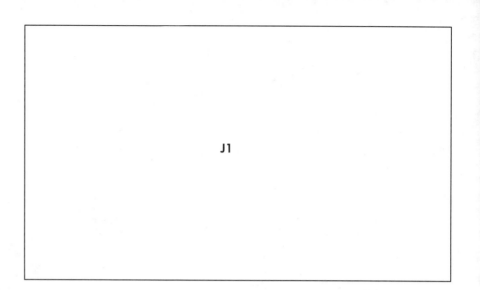

J1

Kentucky Derby Day
8" Block

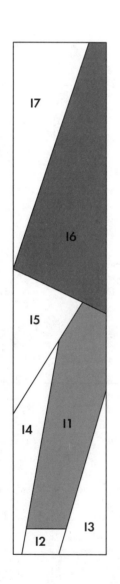

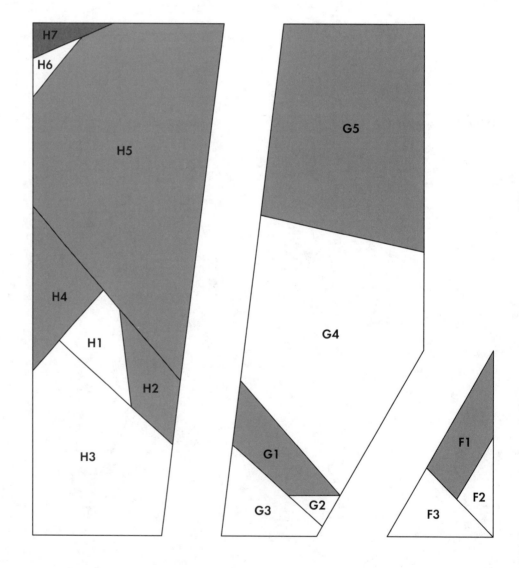

Kentucky Derby Day

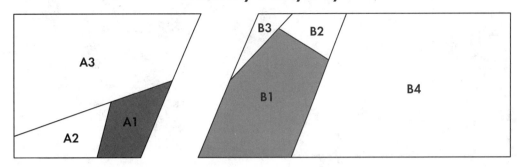

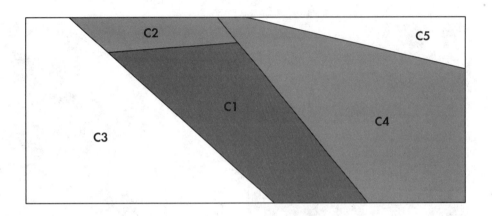

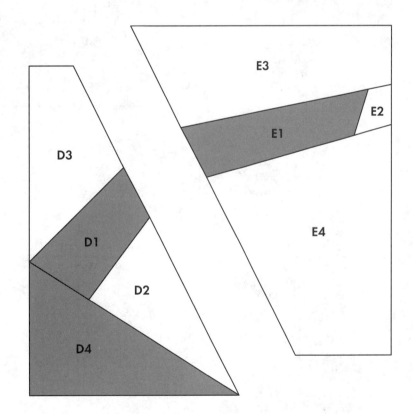

Be Kind To Animals

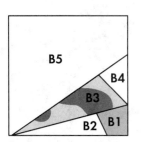

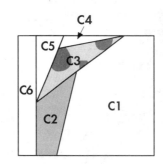

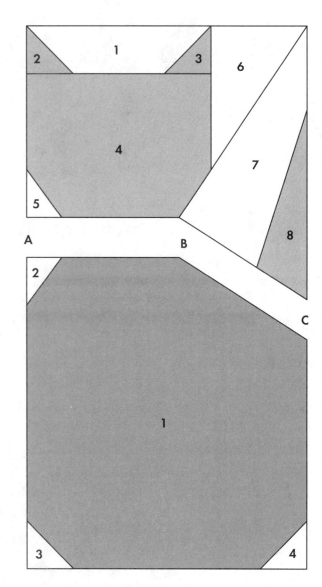

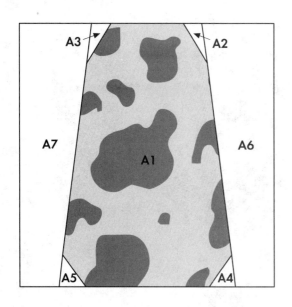

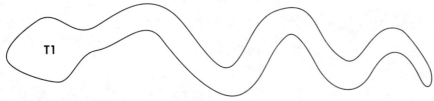

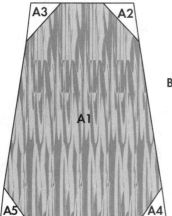

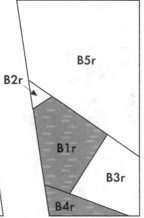

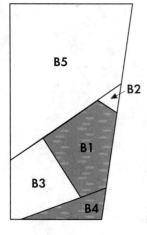

Dog Days of Summer

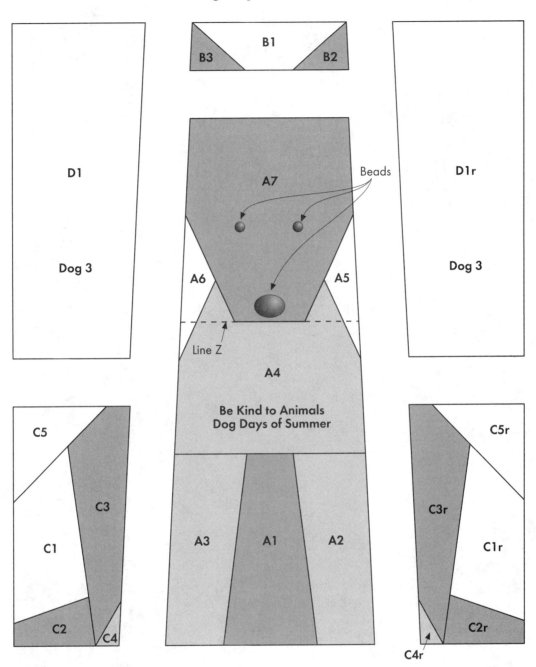

B1
B3   B2

D1

Dog 3

D1r

Dog 3

A7

Beads

A6   A5

Line Z

A4

Be Kind to Animals
Dog Days of Summer

C5

C3

C1

C2   C4

C5r

C3r

C1r

C2r

C4r

A3   A1   A2

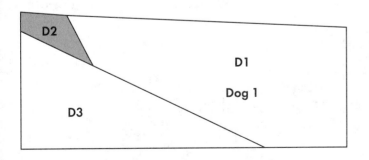

D2

D1

Dog 1

D3

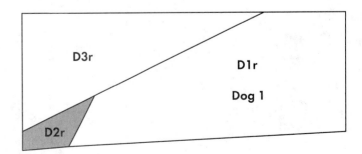

D3r

D1r

Dog 1

D2r

Dog Days of Summer

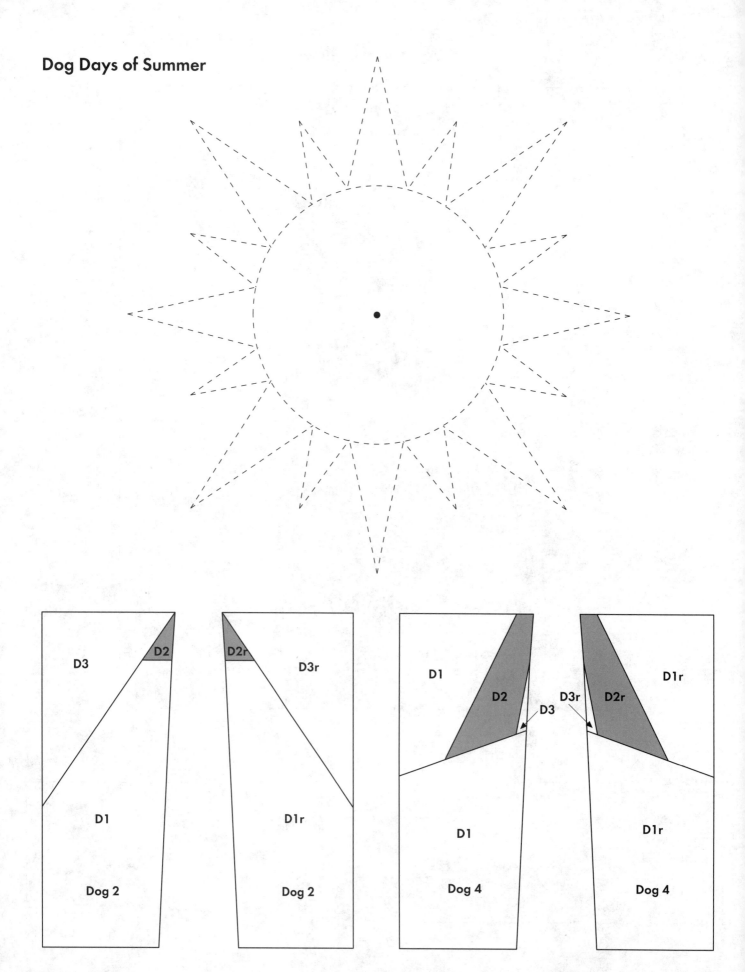

D3 · D2 · D1 · Dog 2

D2r · D3r · D1r · Dog 2

D1 · D2 · D3 · D1 · Dog 4

D3r · D2r · D1r · D1r · Dog 4

Eliza Doolittle Day

Independence Day

Beading design

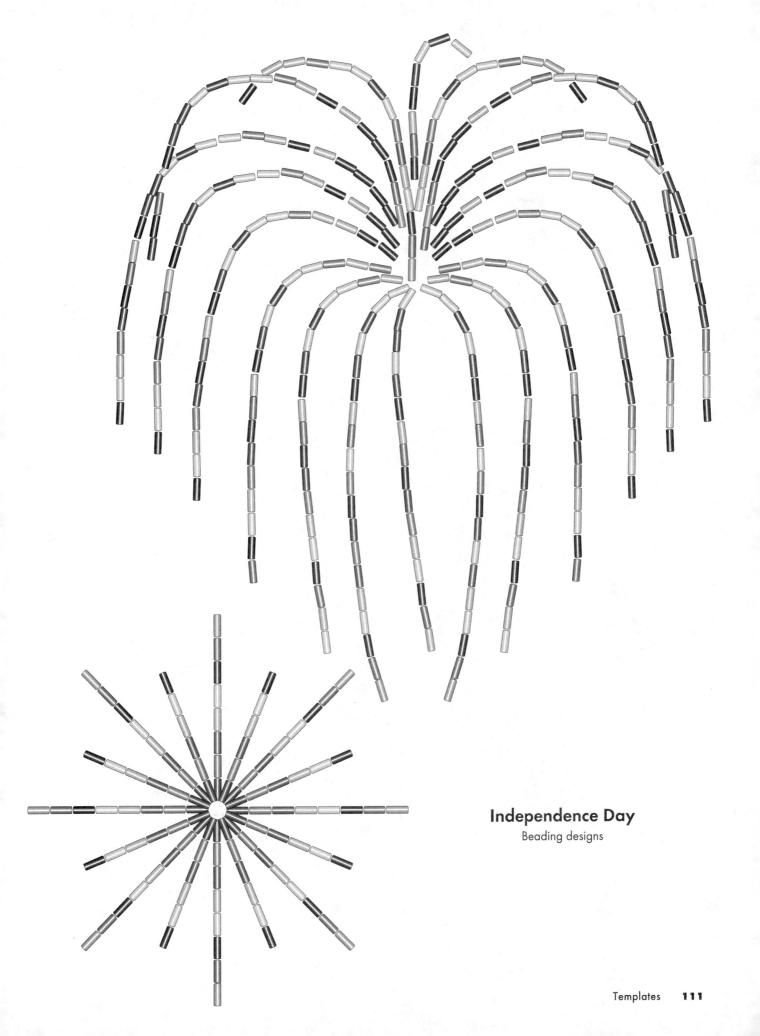

Independence Day

Beading designs

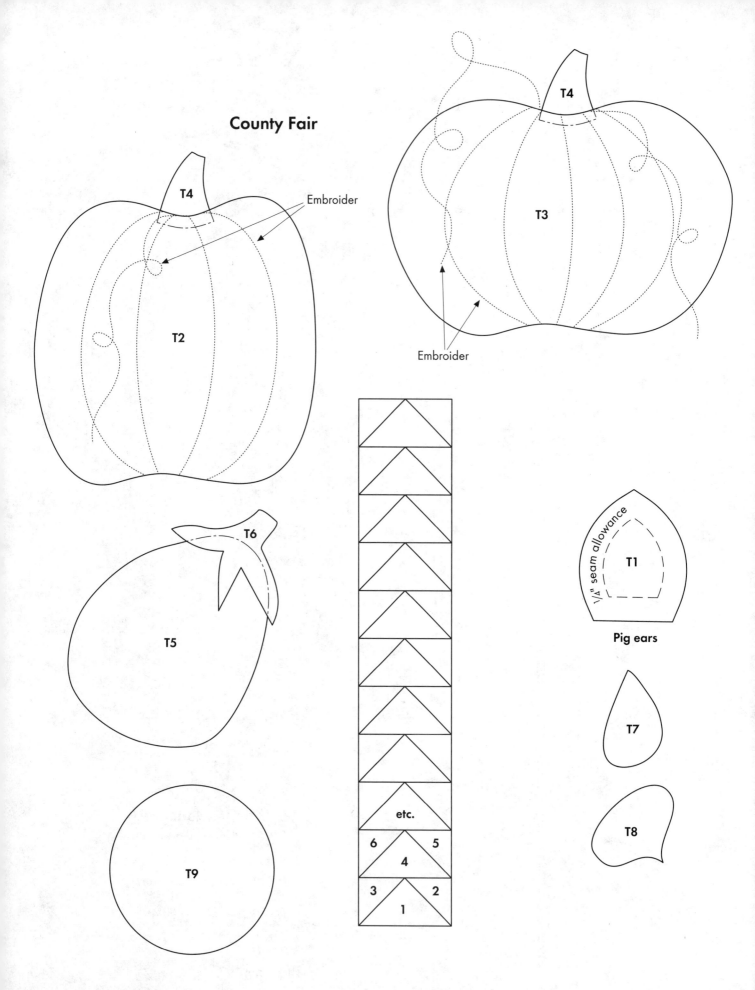

County Fair

T4

Embroider

T2

T4

T3

Embroider

T6

T5

¼" seam allowance

T1

Pig ears

etc.

6		5
4		
3	1	2

T7

T8

T9

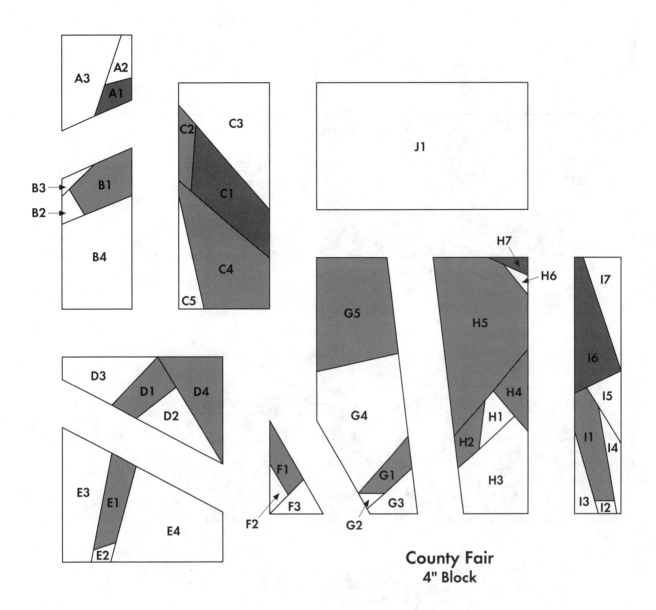

County Fair
4" Block

First Day of School

| E1 | E2 | E3 |

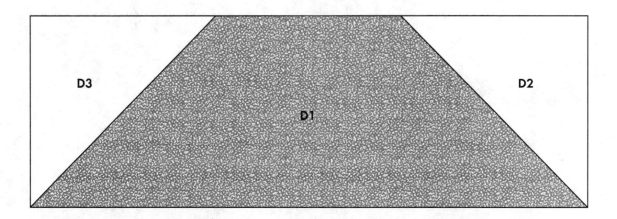

D3   D1   D2

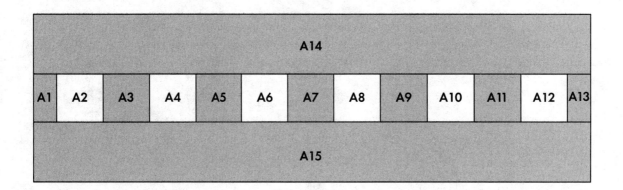

A14

A1 | A2 | A3 | A4 | A5 | A6 | A7 | A8 | A9 | A10 | A11 | A12 | A13

A15

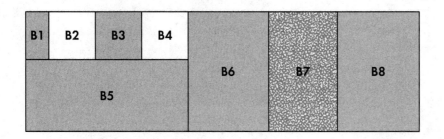

B1 | B2 | B3 | B4 | B5 | B6 | B7 | B8

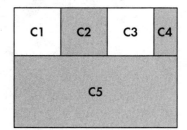

C1 | C2 | C3 | C4 | C5

Boss's Day

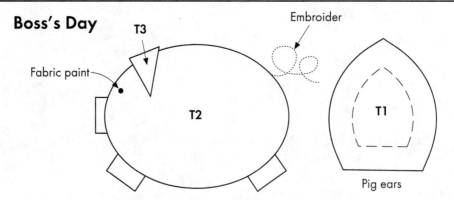

T3

Embroider

Fabric paint

T2

T1

Pig ears

First Day of School

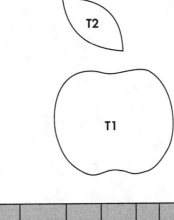

T2

T1

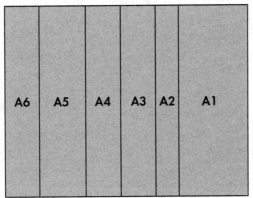

A6 A5 A4 A3 A2 A1

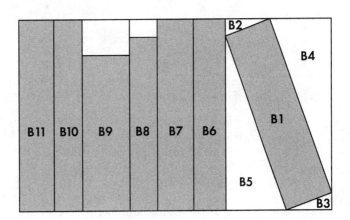

B11 B10 B9 B8 B7 B6 B2 B4 B1 B5 B3

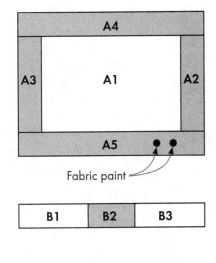

A4

A3 A1 A2

A5

Fabric paint

B1 B2 B3

C1 C2 C3

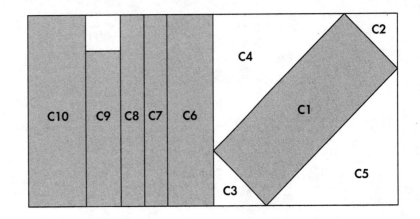

C10 C9 C8 C7 C6 C4 C2 C1 C5 C3

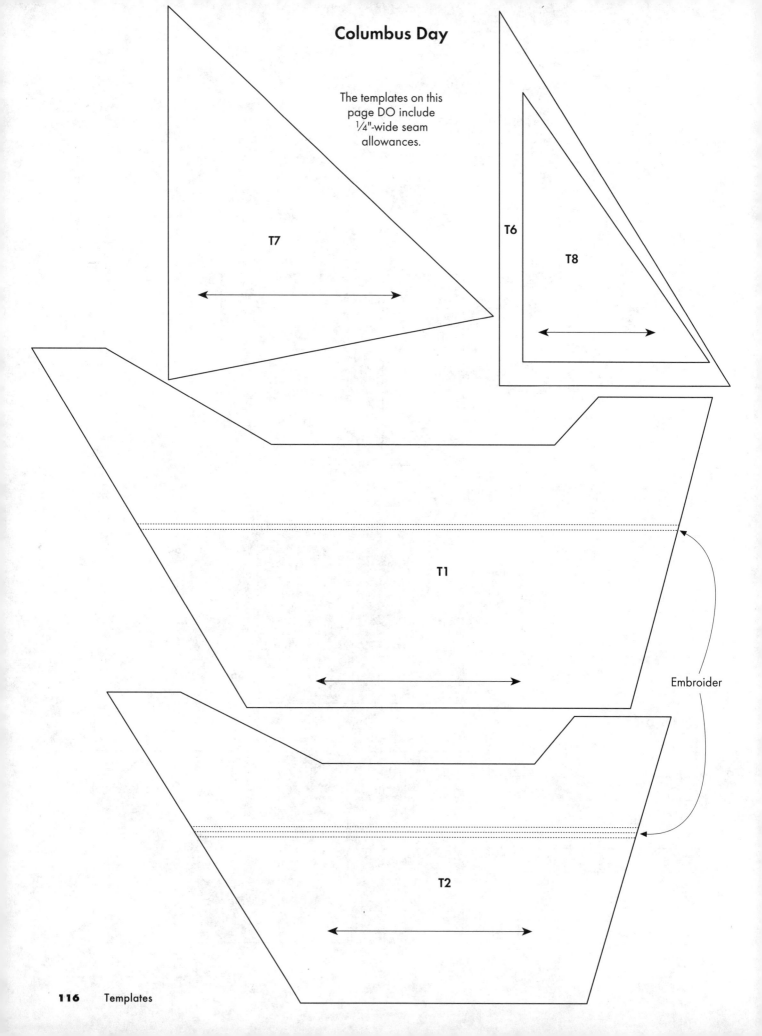

Columbus Day

The templates on this page DO include ¼"-wide seam allowances.

T7

T6

T8

T1

T2

Embroider

Columbus Day

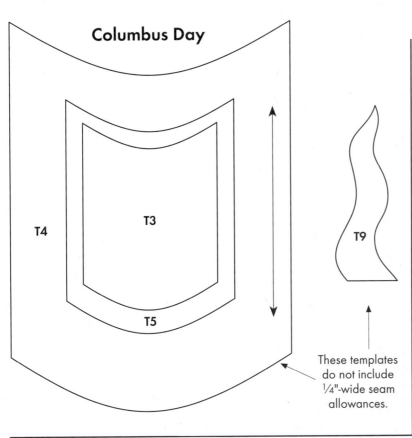

T4

T3

T5

T9

These templates do not include ¼"-wide seam allowances.

Falling Leaves

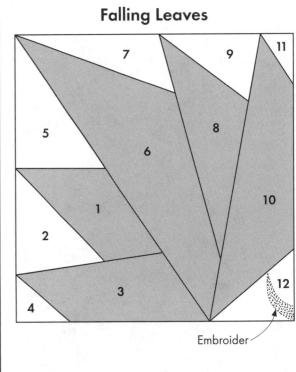

7   9   11

5   8

6

1

2   10

3

4   12

Embroider

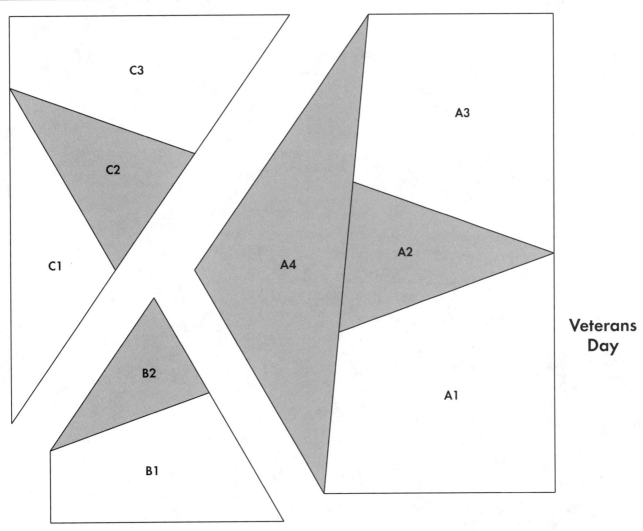

C3

C2

C1

B2

B1

A3

A2

A4

A1

Veterans Day

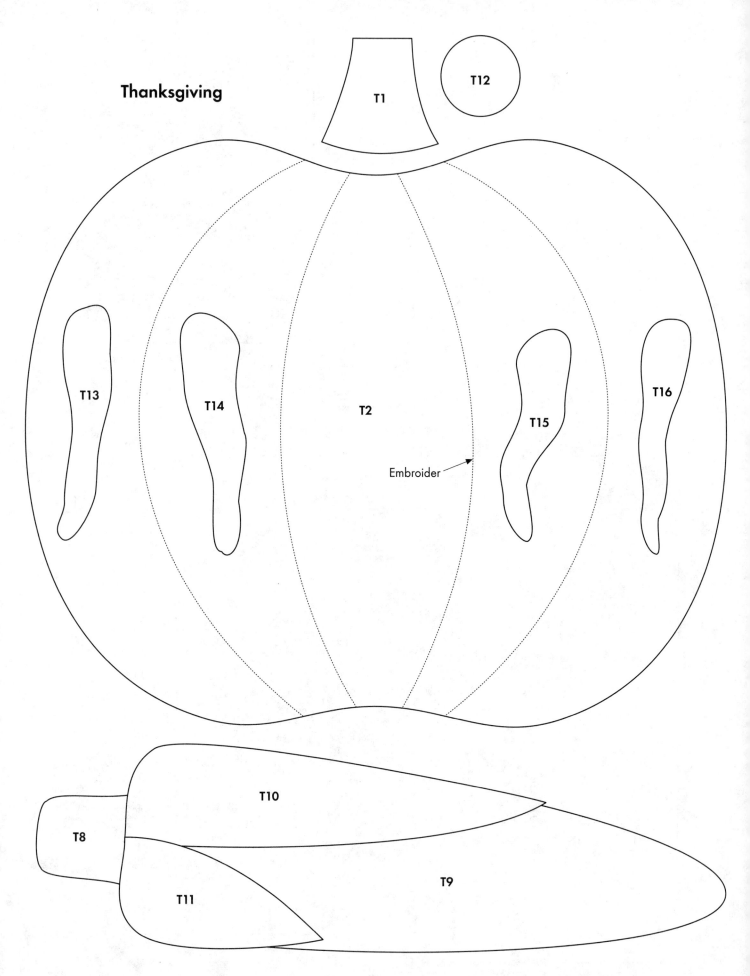

Thanksgiving

T1

T12

T13

T14

T2

Embroider

T15

T16

T10

T8

T11

T9

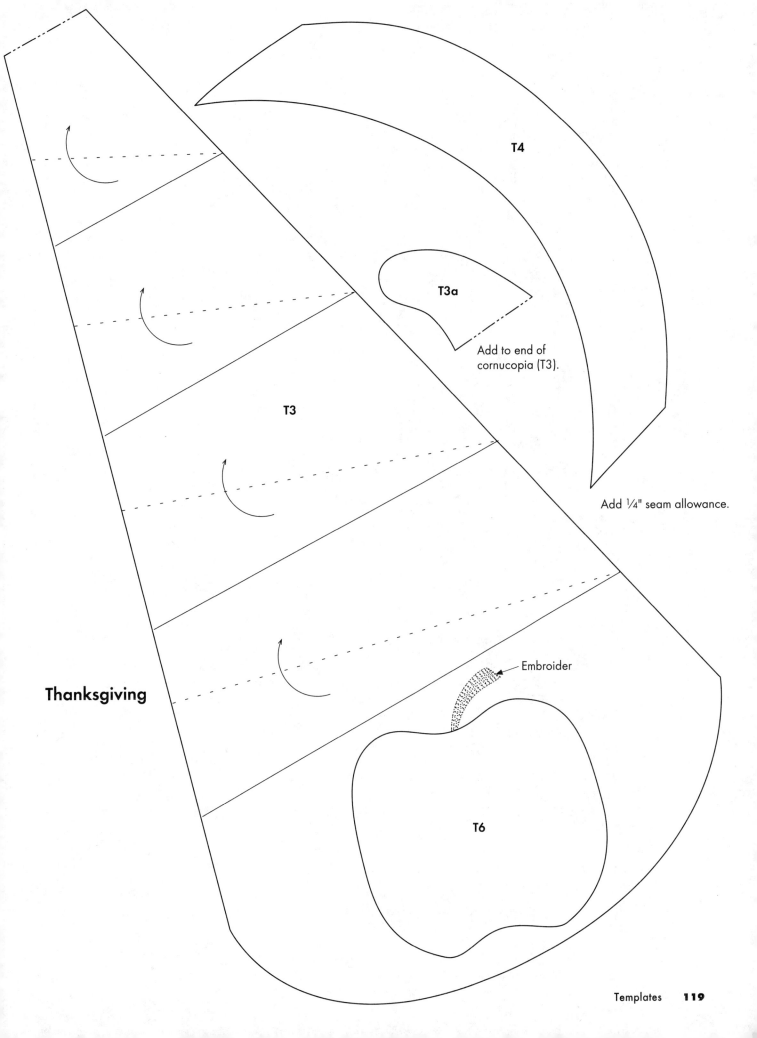

T4

T3a

Add to end of
cornucopia (T3).

T3

Add ¼" seam allowance.

Thanksgiving

Embroider

T6

St. Lucia Day

T2

T1

Embroider

Holly Wreath

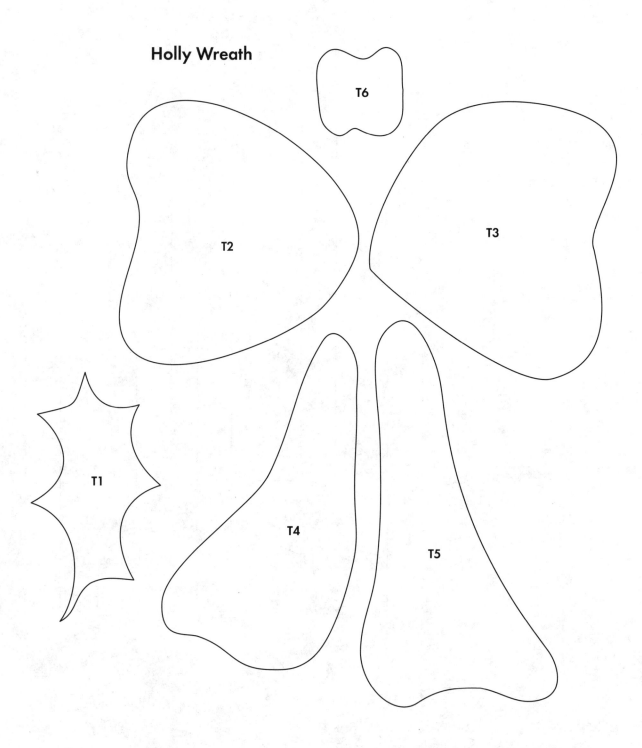

T6

T2

T3

T1

T4

T5

Snow Flurries

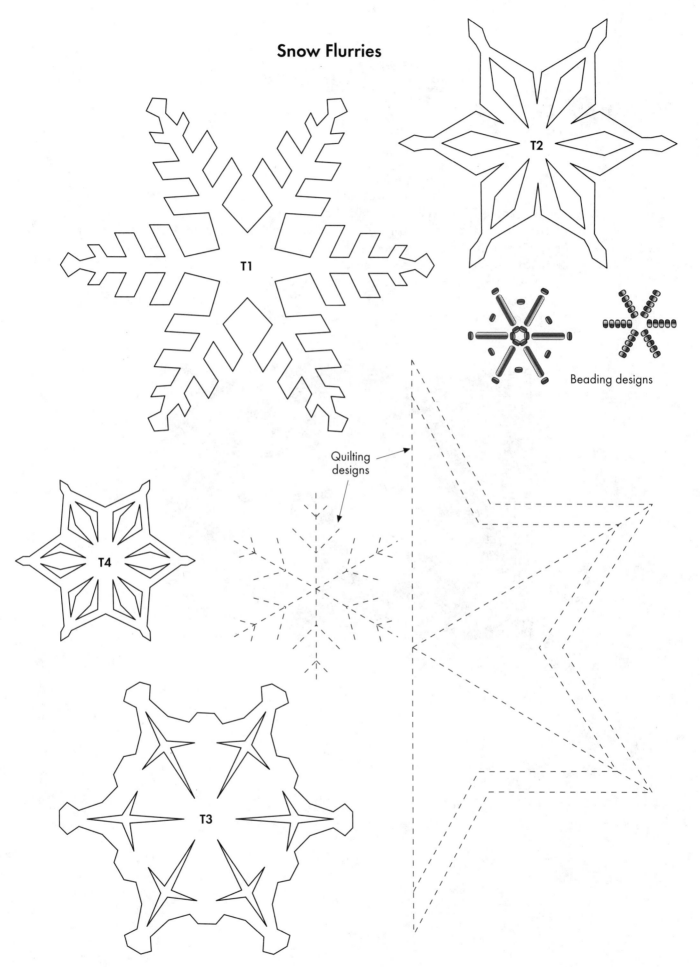

T1

T2

Beading designs

Quilting designs

T4

T3

Meet the Author

Janet Kime teaches and lectures about quiltmaking throughout the Pacific Northwest and edits the newsletter for her local quilt guild, Needle and I. She has written two other books for That Patchwork Place: *Quilts to Share* and *The Cat's Meow*. In this, her third book, she continues to explore her first love in quiltmaking: pieced animal designs.

In addition to her busy schedule of quilting activities, Janet is employed full-time as an academic counselor at the University of Washington in Seattle. She and her goats and cats live on rural Vashon Island.